Rights and Wrongs in the College Classroom

Rights and Wrongs in the College Classroom
Ethical Issues in Postsecondary Teaching

Jordy Rocheleau and Bruce W. Speck
Austin Peay State University

ANKER PUBLISHING COMPANY, INC.
Bolton, Massachusetts

Rights and Wrongs in the College Classroom
Ethical Issues in Postsecondary Teaching

ISBN 978-1-933371-14-6

Composition by Jessica Holland
Cover design by Thomjon Borges

Anker Publishing Company, Inc.
563 Main Street
P.O. Box 249
Bolton, MA 01740-0249 USA

www.ankerpub.com

Library of Congress Cataloging-in-Publication Data

Rocheleau, Jordy.
  Rights and wrongs in the college classroom : ethical issues in postsecondary teaching / Jordy Rocheleau and Bruce W. Speck.
    p. cm.
  Includes bibliographical references and index.
  ISBN 978-1-933371-14-6
  1. College teachers—Professional ethics. 2. College teaching—Moral and ethical aspects. I. Speck, Bruce W. II. Title.

  LB1779.R55 2007
  174.9'37812—dc22
                              2006034607

About the Authors

Jordy Rocheleau is associate professor of philosophy at Austin Peay State University in Clarksville, Tennessee, where he teaches courses in ethics and contemporary philosophy. He received his Ph.D. in philosophy at Michigan State University, with a dissertation on the political implications and viability of Jurgen Habermas' discourse ethic. His publications include articles on the future of critical theory, the implications of political liberalism, democratic approaches to environmental problems, the nature of racial justice, and the role of recognition in politics. Rocheleau turned his attention to educational ethics after teaching a course in professional ethics to future teachers seeking their certification at Austin Peay. He has also served as a Volunteer In Service to America with a literacy consortium and taught English in Costa Rica. Jordy lives with his wife, Miyo Kachi, and cat, Smokey. He is looking forward to having his commitment to ethical education tested afresh in the near future by the arrival of a first child.

Bruce W. Speck is provost and vice president for academic and student affairs at Austin Peay State University (APSU). At APSU he teaches a course in leadership ethics in the President's Emerging Leaders Program. He has served as dean of the College of Arts and Sciences and associate vice chancellor for academic affairs and professor of English at the University of North Carolina–Pembroke; acting director of the Center for Academic Excellence, professor in the Department of English, and coordinator of the writing-across-the-curriculum program at the University of Memphis. He was an assistant professor in the Department of English and Linguistics at Indiana University–Purdue University at Fort Wayne. In addition, he worked in industry as a technical writer. He has published two monographs, *Facilitating Students' Collaborative Writing* (Jossey-Bass, 2002) and *Grading Students' Classroom Writing:*

Issues and Strategies (Jossey-Bass, 2000); coedited nine volumes, including *Spirituality in Higher Education* (Jossey-Bass, 2006); *Service-Learning: History, Theory, and Issues* (Praeger, 2004); *Identifying and Preparing Academic Leaders* (Jossey-Bass, 2004); *Assessment Strategies for the On-Line Class: From Theory to Practice* (Jossey-Bass, 2002); *Approaches to Teaching Non-Native English Speakers Across the Curriculum* (Jossey-Bass, 1997); authored or coauthored six book-length annotated bibliographies for Greenwood Press; and authored 13 book chapters and authored or coauthored 47 articles.

Table of Contents

Introduction

In the preface to his book on academic ethics, Cahn says "some years ago I was asked to deliver a lecture on the subject of 'Ethics in the Academic World.' When I mentioned the topic to a faculty colleague, he remarked, 'It'll be a short talk'" (1986, p. xi).

The remark evokes commonplace views of university professors as being, at best, morally indifferent and, at worst, corrupt and lecherous abusers of the protection of the tenure system. Of course, the comment might be construed differently as implying that a talk on academic ethics would be short because little needs to be said. Those who hold the latter view tend to argue that there are few pressing ethical decisions to be made in the academic world, that any ethical decisions involved are relatively straightforward, and that faculty judgment is sufficient to deal with any issues that arise.

These two prevalent, but mutually contradictory, views of faculty are reflected in the title of Cahn's book, *Saints and Scamps*, which implies that faculty tend to be either incorruptible or incorrigible. Surely this is a false dichotomy. Most faculty are neither so indifferent or opposed to ethical judgment as to warrant the label "scamps" nor so firmly virtuous and clear in their ethical principles as to merit sainthood. In addition to implausibility, the portrayals of faculty as either incorruptible or incorrigible share the implication that there is little need for reflection about the ethics of teaching. If faculty are generally morally unconcerned or corrupt, then any discussion of faculty obligations would be useless, insofar as it will fall on deaf ears and have no hope of securing compliance. Conversely, if faculty as a matter of course comprehended and observed all their professional obligations, it would be unnecessary to analyze and make recommendations regarding the moral decisions they confront. However, if faculty are both corruptible and corrigible, as we suggest is

ʾsis of moral issues and principles for the conduct of
ʾul and necessary.

‿ann's (1986) book (and a handful of others), the literature
ᴖɪɪ academic ethics is relatively small. The ethics of the teaching profession
have been given less systematic analysis than those of other professions.
Classes in medical, business, environmental, and journalism ethics are
common in universities. But ethicists, who are largely college professors,
have devoted little of their critical energy to the analysis of their own profession. We examine some reasons for this paucity of educational ethics literature not only to explain this phenomenon, but also to acknowledge and
confront objections to writing a book on this subject and to clarify the purpose and scope of our work.

There are at least four reasons why the ethics of academics receives
little attention. First, in many ways, academic life assumes that professors
will be ethical. There is reason to think that those who go into teaching
are bright and well-meaning people who ought to be able to figure out
what is right and wrong and be motivated to do the former and avoid the
latter. College professors commonly choose their profession less for personal profit than out of love for the pursuit of knowledge and commitment to its development through education. The personal love of and
commitment to education's mission provides more reason to take the
ethics of faculty conduct for granted than, say, business professionals, in
which the central goal of profit is in frequent tension with ethical norms.

However, to rely on the generally good intentions of faculty is to fail
to notice a few things. First, regardless of one's motives for entering the
teaching profession, incentives can arise to cut corners within the teaching process—as when one has to allocate time between class preparation,
research, and recreation. Additionally, regardless of how well-intentioned
one is, ethical dilemmas arise. For example, professors have to decide
whether and to what extent to grade on a curve, befriend students, or
advocate their moral and political views in the classroom. Good intentions do not provide sufficient guidance to answer such questions—in
which professors face a choice not between self-interest and moral obligations, but between conflicting ethical principles and values. Like other professionals providing a service, educators must make choices in which fundamental principles conflict. For example, the duty to respect individual

autonomy frequently contrasts with the duty to foster the well-being of one's client or the good of society as a whole. An analysis of the ethical obligations of professors, and the moral dilemmas which they face, can help professors understand what values are at stake and make better decisions when confronted with dilemmas.

A second reason for the relative paucity of literature on educational ethics is that educational issues are considered less pressing than those which deal with sensational news-grabbing themes. Medical ethics courses take up health care access, assisted suicide, and abortion. Public policy courses address the justification of war and the death penalty. Business and journalism ethics have their own links into national debates via fraudulent accounting, embezzlement, and false reporting scandals. By contrast, course content and grading practices rarely get national attention, nor does the quality of professors' relationships with their students unless sex is involved. Yet despite its lack of press attention and dearth of hot button issues, university teaching is of ethical and social import. Ethical judgments must be made about fairness in evaluation, how to respond to an offensive student, and whether professors may date former students. How professors make such judgments and how they respond to such dilemmas affects the lives of students. Professors have considerable influence and authority in the classroom and generally are given the trust of students. Such power can be used to foster student growth, independence, and well-being, but it can also be misused. Collectively, university teaching has a formative influence on the nature of citizenry and the health of democracy. Judgments about conduct in teaching can be made for the better or worse and systematic analysis of such issues and recommended principles for addressing them can help faculty decision-making and improve conduct.

A third reason for lack of professorial ethics literature is that statements of moral and professional obligations are thought to be at odds with academic freedom. Professors' freedom of inquiry is sometimes thought to imply that academics have carte blanche in their teaching practices and institutional roles. The legal protection of tenure would seem to make ethical demands upon professors invalid for any practical purpose. However, to view academic freedom and ethics as incompatible is to misunderstand both. Not only are there reasonable limits to academic freedom, but professors are also obligated to use their freedom responsibly and effectively even when sanctions are inapplicable. Far from making ethical prescriptions irrelevant, the awarding of tenure presupposes and relies upon an ethically committed faculty.

However, outside of the legal issues about academic freedom and tenure, many deny whether ethical goals and principled constraints are valid in education, a fourth obstacle to systematic reflection on academic ethics. Libertarian approaches to education question whether education is a moral endeavor to be constrained and guided by ethical norms. The push for separating morality and education today comes from both the left and right of the political spectrum. On the left, postmodernists suspect that ethical norms are mere exercises of power. Norms which regulate academic life are seen as particularly constraining of human potential. Others (liberal and conservative alike) oppose centralized control over the goals and means of education, fearing excessive government control and loss of independence in inquiry. Contemporary conservative critics of education are particularly suspicious of campaigns to promote ethics in the classroom, on the grounds that educators are prone to promote disproportionately their liberal ideals of social and economic equality, individual freedom, and pacifism. From this perspective, efforts to prescribe and regulate faculty conduct have been derided as inculcating a "political correctness" which stifles intellectual discourse.

Further disabling ethical recommendations in the academy are economic constraints. Universities are faced with ever-tightening budgets. Educational policymakers, funders, and administrators increasingly embrace a business model in which university energies are employed to produce student credit hours as efficiently as possible and to produce saleable products, such as licenses and patents. When profitability and financial efficiency become higher education's guiding principles, other ethical goals—such as depth of learning, independence in inquiry, and quality professor-student relationships—become so many luxuries and barriers to a university's productivity.

Yet refusal to talk about teaching as a moral endeavor is unfortunate. As Hauerwas (1995) argues, education has moral effects whether these consequences are consciously promoted or not: "The failure of the modern university is not that those teaching in it fail to shape students morally, but that they fail to take responsibility for doing so" (p. 35). The imposition of ethical principles by policy or social pressure must be balanced with the value of freedom of inquiry. However, to abandon moral constraints and ethical guidance and trust entirely the whims of instructor choice or market efficiency is irresponsible. If, as we argue, some general principles are defensible as obligatory for all educators and are helpful in guiding conduct in individual cases, then education is better and morally sounder if these principles are understood, respected, and promoted.

We will add to the literature on academic ethics by both exploring issues and outlining faculty duties regarding teaching students at the university level. We will analyze ethical issues that occur in instruction at the postsecondary level, including relationships with students, such as evaluation and advisement. With this focus we set aside other moral issues which face university faculty, such as the ethics of research and problematic relationships with one's colleagues and institution. We address these other relationships and spheres of academic life insofar as they are related to faculty obligations regarding the teaching and advising of students. By providing an ethical framework for assessing ethical issues in teaching and making responsible decisions, we will have contributed to a comprehensive understanding of academic ethics.

In the six chapters that follow we begin by discussing the ethics of teaching generally, and then analyze particular dilemmas that faculty face. Thus, Chapter 1 lays out a basic conception of ethical obligations in college teaching. It discusses the moral grounds of professors' teaching duties, outlines principles that ought to govern university instruction, and responds in greater detail to objections to an ethic of teaching.

In Chapter 2 we address the issue of advocacy—questioning whether, to what extent, and in what manner professors ought to promote their beliefs and values in the classroom. We address concerns about faculty interference with student freedom of inquiry, and discuss the meaning and nature of indoctrination. Ultimately we give a conditional endorsement of limited classroom advocacy.

Chapter 3 discusses conflicts of interest which can undermine teaching ethics. We analyze a range of ways in which academics' personal interest may interfere with their duties as professors. Discussing issues such as the extent to which research may be chosen over teaching and whether faculty may assign their own books in their courses, we give ethical guidance for faculty in negotiating such conflicts.

Chapter 4 addresses ethical issues in student evaluation, including the ethical purposes of grading and the sense in which grades can and should be objective. We discuss problems in and principles for fair and effective assignment construction as well as evaluation.

In Chapter 5 we discuss the nature of respectful treatment of students. We explore the ethical basis and meaning of the demand to treat students respectfully, its implications for professor conduct that is offensive to students, and causes of faculty disrespect of students.

Chapter 6 deals with intimate relationships between faculty and students. We begin with a consideration of romantic and sexual relationships between professor and student. We then explore what makes such relationships problematic and under what conditions faculty are obligated to avoid them. The second half of the chapter takes up the issue of friendship between faculty and students. We consider whether friendship with students is appropriate for faculty and whether it might be a relationship model that faculty ought to strive to achieve with students.

We conclude by noting conditions that affect the realization of a faculty code of ethics. We discuss the need for both institutional and faculty support of a code of ethics, and argue that the cultivation and observance of a teaching ethic has intrinsic rewards for faculty as individuals and professionals.

This volume is the product of two authors who share certain perspectives on educational ethics, but at times take differing perspectives. Although we have engaged in discussion and revisions to present theses and arguments that we both believe have merit, we have nevertheless allowed each other freedom to make statements that as individuals we might frame differently. Thus we disclose that the primary responsibilities for writing Chapters 1, 2, and 6 were Jordy's, and the primary responsibilities for writing Chapters 3, 4, and 5 were Bruce's. However, we both claim ownership of the volume as a joint effort.

Any publishing project requires assistance from various people, including publishers, editors, and reviewers. Before sending our manuscript to the publisher, we received excellent advice for revising from Heidi Speck (who gave valuable feedback that was most helpful in revising particular chapters) and Carmen Speck (who read the manuscript with a critical eye for catching various errors that we had missed in writing the chapters). Jordy would like to thank above all his wife, Miyo Kachi, who provided valuable comments on his chapters and invaluable loving support and patient understanding as the project moved from conception to fruition.

We hope that readers will find the positions we have taken useful as they consider the ethical import of professorial relations in the teaching enterprise.

Academic Ethics: Sources, Principles, and Responses to Objections

While texts and courses about ethical issues in medicine and business have proliferated in the last 20 years, there has been comparatively little discussion of the ethics of college education itself. This may be because the stakes in college classrooms appear relatively small. Unlike the hospital, lives generally are not in danger. And unlike corporate decision-makers, college professors do not control millions of dollars of goods (Markie, 1994).

Nonetheless, what professors do matters and is of ethical import. Teaching affects the lives of students and, by educating future citizens and workers, affects the well-being of society as a whole. Good, thoughtful, engaged teaching leads to better education and hence more informed individuals and social progress. At the same time, thoughtless words, mistaken grades, or misconduct by professors can harm students and hinder their ability to contribute to society.

Educational ethics may also gain less attention than business and medical ethics because professors appear to have straightforward obligations, free of the type of dilemmas that arise for medical and business practitioners. Professors, it seems, simply have to show up for their classes, teach them well, grade appropriately, and then do independent research on the side. Unlike business professionals who are selling services, educators do not have to choose as directly between self-interest and obligations to others. Business and medicine involves historic conflicts between consumers, practitioners, and business owners, which result in ethical dilemmas for the professional. Scarce resources, such as hospital beds and livers, have to be allocated. Important ethical principles, such as individual autonomy and health, have conflicting implications. This results in ethical dilemmas in which difficult and sometimes tragic choices must be made. We don't normally think of educators as having to choose between competing values and interests.

ical dilemmas and tensions in education are less readily ap. but they are nonetheless present. Professors do have to choose between personal interest and the well-being of their students, as when professors must decide how much time to dedicate to teaching as opposed to research. Professors also have to choose between various interests and values, as when they must decide between allowing students freedom to pursue their own interests and the provision of structure designed to teach what is thought most important. No matter how well-meaning or skilled a professor is, he or she faces ethical dilemmas—whether to grade on a curve or fixed scale, how severely to punish cheating, and how to take into account his or her own values in course curriculum construction. Although such ethical dilemmas are seldom discussed in books—much less television dramas—they are real, and professors experience them regularly.

It has been widely noted that professors receive little pedagogical training; the credential for teaching is the terminal degree in the discipline one will teach. The lack of pedagogical training also involves a lack of training to deal with ethical issues. Many instructors will analyze ethical dilemmas for themselves or discuss them with trusted colleagues. Others respond by sticking to long-formed teaching habits, learned from their own esteemed former professors. When they recognize dilemmas, facing time pressure and unsure of how to resolve these issues or whom to consult, professors are apt to simply use their intuitive judgment of what seems the right thing to do. Teaching involves little direct supervision, so it is possible for professors to engage in questionable ethical practices for years without being confronted. In any case, the ethics of teaching could benefit from more systematic reflection. We will describe the nature of faculty teaching obligations and the ethical dilemmas that arise in teaching, and provide suggestions for resolving these ethical issues.

Academic Ethics as an Instance of Morality

In one sense academic ethics could be simply understood as a particular instance of morality. It is widely accepted that humans have mutual obligations and ought to follow basic principles in their interactions.

Basic moral principles include respecting others, nonmaleficence (refraining from harming others), fidelity (telling the truth and keeping promises), and beneficence (fostering the common good) (Ross, 1930). Such principles apply no less to professors in their dealings with students. Professors should refrain from assaulting or abusing students. Professors have a positive obligation to show respect to their students as well as other individuals, tolerating their views and not interfering with their freedom of action. Principles of honesty imply that professors should sincerely profess what they take to be correct views and should keep promises made to students. The duty of beneficence implies that, as humans, we ought to do things that contribute to the greater good. Professors find themselves in the arena of the classroom and, therefore, should act in this role to contribute to the well-being of students and society. Academic ethics in this sense is nothing more than the application of these general principles to the circumstance of education.

While these principles capture some of the moral duties that professors have, they certainly do not completely exhaust these obligations. Professors have obligations stemming from their role as professors aside from those of an ordinary citizen or bystander. Professors have obligations of beneficence, respect, and truthfulness beyond those of decent humanity. While the ordinary citizen may have some obligation to help others, it is generally not considered a duty to help others with their problems or answer their questions, though professors are obligated to take pains to do exactly this. Professors have a special duty to attempt to help their students. Professors are not expected just to not lie to their students, but also to teach courses in a way which best facilitates student learning of their subjects. While it is accepted that we will display favoritism in our daily lives, professors are supposed to treat and evaluate their students impartially. These sorts of obligations show that teaching involves its own particular moral commitments beyond ordinary interpersonal moral obligations.

Legal and Contractual Obligations

Some of the obligations specific to professors are expressed in the employment contract. By accepting a teaching position, a professor promises to fulfill various ends; normally these specify teaching duties as well as expectations for research and service. Contracts typically specify that professors are to meet with students regularly, make office hours available, hand out a syllabus, teach material relevant to the description in the course catalogue, and submit grades for each student at the end of the term. Contracts may also proscribe other conduct—for example, prohibiting financial or sexual relationships with students, or requiring additional types of communication with students (such as notifying them of their midterm grades and contacting advisees about registration deadlines).

Yet the employment contract and the laws governing teaching do not completely subsume the obligations of professors. There are obligations which are not, and frequently could not or should not be, expressed contractually. If Professor Smith is ill-prepared for class and responds to students' concerns in an unhelpful and uncaring manner, Smith may fulfill the technical requirements of his contract but nonetheless be guilty of unethical conduct. Good teaching requires going beyond the minimal legal and contractual obligations to one's institution, showing concern for the individual needs of students, improving lesson plans, and treating students fairly and respectfully. Nor is this necessarily a shortcoming of the contract itself. It would be difficult to specify exactly what good teaching or fair treatment of students entails. A legal document can only require a minimal standard of treatment—including refraining from obvious forms of misconduct and abuse—but cannot specify and require an ideal level of teaching. Such terms are difficult to define and involve much context-sensitive judgment, which is not readily written in a contract. Some ethical obligations are better understood informally and extralegally.

To make all instructors' ethical obligations into legal obligations would also be a great intrusion of law and contract into everyday relationships which are largely a matter of individual contextual judgment. If one were bound by law to treat others respectfully, one would be open to numerous lawsuits. Speech and interaction would be stifled as instructors worried about whether they crossed the line of respectfulness. We are familiar with ethical obligations that are not legally embodied: It is generally understood that one ought not lie, break promises, commit adultery, exhibit crudeness, be thoughtless, or show intolerance, but the breaches of these rules are not legally punishable.

Additionally, laws and contracts themselves should have an ethical basis. Contracts and laws only tell us what the rules currently are but not what they should be. This is particularly obvious when contracts come into question or are being rewritten. There must be reasons, beyond the existence of the contracts and laws, for the existence of such strictures. If the terms of the employment contract warrant faculty observance and public support, they must be defensible. In order to decide whether the rules are good and how they can be improved, other ethical principles must be referenced and other ethical arguments made.

Not only are contracts not a complete expression of teaching obligations, but it is also questionable whether laws and employee rules should always be followed. Instructors may have good reason to think that the rules are wrong or have exceptions. Consider situations such as these:

- Campus policy requires that students caught plagiarizing be given failing grades for the course. A professor finds a case of plagiarism in which the student, who normally seems dedicated and honest, may have been confused about campus policy. Should the student be given an F according to policy or given a lesser penalty?

- An instructor agrees to teach courses of a particular description but believes the courses would be of more value if some material was replaced by different subjects. Should the professor teach according to the course catalogue or teach the material she believes is most valuable?

- Campus rules forbid minors or nonstudents from entering a classroom, but local K–12 public schools have been cancelled. Many college students who have children are unable to find last-minute child care. They would like to bring their children to

class and have them work quietly. Should a professor follow policy and forbid entry to the children or make an exception?

- Some state laws require that educators report any information
  that they have about sexual assaults. A student asks a faculty
  member if she may confide in her. After securing a promise of
  confidentiality, the student tells the faculty member of a past sexual assault. The student has shared this in order to discuss her
  past and not because of any concern about continuing danger.
  Should the faculty member break confidentiality and report the
  student's experience as the law requires?

In such cases, when the professor disagrees with the rules or believes
exceptions should be made to them, a dilemma arises. There is some duty
to do what one takes to be inherently right separate from what the rules
stipulate, but exactly when the rules should be overridden is not transparent. If there are times when one's duty to conscience outweighs our
obligation to obey, there are also times when one should follow what one
thinks are imperfect rules for the sake of fulfilling promises and maintaining order. Nonetheless, such cases show that knowledge of contractual obligations does not exhaust the ethical obligations of instructors or
resolve their ethical dilemmas.

Extracontractual Obligations

As noted above, a professor's role includes obligations beyond those
explicitly required in the contract. These obligations can be understood
as stemming from an implicit social contract that professors have with
their students, employers, and society in general. There are certain reciprocal obligations that various members of society must fulfill if these relationships are to work. Although such obligations are not written down or
even necessarily explicitly understood, they are obligations that citizens
would recognize they expect of others and are obligated to follow themselves (Chambers, 1983; Rawls, 1971).

First, students enter classes with an understanding that professors will teach certain subject matter adequately and that professors will treat them in a fair manner. Professors, by presenting themselves as professionals knowledgeable in their subject matter and committed to the impartial pursuit of truth, have an obligation to fulfill this role (even if no explicit promise is made in the employment contract). True, the syllabi that instructors give students can be seen as a kind of contract: Professors promise to do certain things such as hold office hours; cover subjects X, Y, and Z; and grade on the basis of the quality of a student's work. But some obligations to teach truthfully, fairly, and diligently would exist without such an explicit promise. Professors not only present themselves as knowledgeable but also rely on students' trust in and respect of this knowledge in order to teach classes. The authority given to and presumed by professors presupposes that this authority will be used responsibly.

Professorial obligations are also implied by the formal powers and freedoms given to academics. Instructors have the ability to give grades and grant degrees. In exchange for this power, it is understood that professors will use it reasonably, fairly, and honestly. Grades and degrees are not to be conferred on those who have not earned them. Admittance into the profession also implies that professors take up a commitment to the pursuit of knowledge. While this may most directly imply that professors should attempt to conduct meaningful and honest research, the pursuit of truth is also relevant in the classroom. To not attempt to promote and pursue knowledge in the classroom would be a wrong committed against one's profession as well as one's students.

The obligations of professors go beyond duties to their students, universities, and professions. Academics, it could be argued, have an obligation to society as a whole. Most academics are beneficiaries of social support—teachers at state schools are paid in part with tax dollars. Private schools also frequently benefit from state funding as well. Besides their salaries, society also accords professors freedoms. Professors are accorded academic freedom not just to pursue their own research agendas, but also to design and teach courses according to their own judgment. In particular, the granting of tenure accords faculty an independence felt by few public servants. The granting of such freedom

assumes that it will be used responsibly for the pursuit of truth and benefit of society. While there is significant room for debate about just what
paths of research and teaching further knowledge and social well-being,
the obligation to pursue truth yields responsibilities in the conduct of
teaching and research.

Of course, the exact terms of the social contract are not completely
clear. Professors cannot know exactly what society expects them to
achieve in their teaching. Indeed, individuals in society probably have
not thought through what they expect of the academic profession. This
means that professors can at best ask what society would expect if it artic-
ulated its desires. Even if professors could poll the public to find out what
it desires, such preferences should not necessarily guide academic work.
After all, the public doesn't necessarily understand academic disciplines
or have a vision about the proper role of academic knowledge. The public is likely to favor the satisfaction of material wants and needs over
knowledge for its own sake. Academics have an obligation to pursue and
teach the truth, even if this is in opposition to other social values and
interests.

Presumably, on reflection, the public would ask academics to balance
at least the two different values we have discussed: social utility and truth.
Academics should contribute to both the greater good and the accumulation of knowledge for its own sake. The two are generally mutually
supportive; the possession of knowledge involves an understanding of
and ability to act in the world, which should help the solving of social
problems. Scientific discoveries lead to new forms of technology.
Developments in social science contribute to public policy and the development of consumer goods. Yet there may be forms of knowledge that do
not contribute to the good of society. In particular, abstract theory or
obscure facts about the universe may have little immediate value or
known application. Perhaps even more difficult would be cases in which
knowledge had potentially ill effects for society: historical and sociological theory critical of society or investigations into the future of the earth
or human nature which result in pessimistic conclusions may cause anx-
iety, depression, or anger. Academics, in their teaching as well as research,
may have to choose between the ideal of truth and the ideal of social
beneficence.

In teaching, there is at least one other goal besides those of knowledge and social utility—the development of students as individuals. Of course, this goal is partly implicit in the goals of disseminating knowledge and contributing to social well-being. By fostering student learning and development of useful skills, it could be said that professors are contributing to student development. Nonetheless, the development involved in teaching is not fully subsumed under the goals of truth and utility. Philosophers of education have widely held that education ought to develop mature individuals (Aristotle, 1985; Kant, 1997; Locke, 1693/1997; Plato, 1961). In particular, contemporary educational theorists emphasize that education should contribute to students' development as autonomous moral agents capable of thinking responsibly and creatively for themselves. While sharing knowledge would frequently enhance individual capacity for thought, replacing didactic lecture with open-ended discussion may best promote individual student growth. Similarly, encouraging social utility probably generally implies promoting individual skills which also promote individual development and a wider range of individual choice. There is much to be said for John Stuart Mill's (1859/1989) famous argument that "mankind are greater gainers by suffering each to live as seems good to themselves, than by compelling each to live as seems good to the rest." Nonetheless, the greatest range of individual choice may not always be best for society, particularly in the realm of education. Professors may have to choose between fostering independent student choice and cultivating the kinds of knowledge and intellectual habits thought most true or valuable for society.

Overview of Principles of Academic Ethics

It has been noted that academic ethics has several sources. In addition to the specific rules and laws that apply to them, professors have obligations that arise from basic moral principles and from the goals and ideals of teaching. The intersection of moral principles and the role of teaching creates a unique ethical dynamic. At the same time that instructors have particular goals that they are attempting to further in the classroom (truth, individual development, and utility), they are also constrained by moral principles, such as fidelity and equal respect for persons, in the pursuit of these goals. For example, the principle of equal respect implies that classes should be organized fairly, such that the rewards and benefits received and derived from the class are equally available to all. Students who do similar work should receive similar grades; if extra credit or instructor assistance is offered to one student, it should be offered to others in similar situations, and so on. Of course, the principle of equal respect doesn't rigidly imply that every individual should be treated in the same way or every situation responded to with the same procedure. Aristotle (1985) defined justice as treating like cases alike and different cases differently, thus emphasizing the principle of fairness or equity—in which relevant differences are taken into account. A good paper should be given a different grade than a poor paper. A more serious breach of rules should be given a more serious penalty. A student or class that has difficulty with material should be given additional help, whereas students that are grasping material readily should be encouraged to move on to a different subject. Equitable treatment involves taking into account relevant differences (Strike & Soltis, 1998).

If professors are expected to treat students equitably, they are also supposed to treat students with respect. Though a professor who abused and ridiculed all students would meet the equality provision, the professor would fail to treat students with respect. In the classroom, treating students with respect means not just refraining from physical assault, but also using one's power as an educator to foster—rather than undermine—students' freedom and well-being. Because of their power in the classroom, professors should not ridicule students. Although some amount of negative feedback—in the form of written and verbal comments as well as bad grades—is warranted to motivate education and signal the need for change, punitive measures not designed to benefit student learning are unwarranted. One of the great questions regarding respect for the student and his or her self-determination is whether professors ought to advocate their own conclusions and beliefs in their courses or adopt an impartial stance in order to encourage student independence. What counts as wrongful indoctrination as opposed to the reasonable teaching of relevant material will be a key theme in Chapter 2. For now, we want to emphasize that instructors have a dual obligation to pursue the ethical aims of higher education and to do so in a manner which respects moral principles.

Because there are so many different moral principles and ideals relevant to teaching that potentially conflict with each other, few absolutes can be asserted. The ethics of education are a matter of determining the implications and relative weight of ethical principles in a particular situation. Ultimately what is ethical can only be determined by a context-sensitive judgment which takes into account all relevant moral considerations.

Answering Ethical Relativism

If ethics requires context-sensitive judgments rather than an assertion of absolute principles, the question arises whether there are objectively right conclusions at all in ethics. Any work on ethics must say something about the challenge of ethical relativism, which holds that ethical conduct is a matter of personal preference or opinion because there are no objectively right answers (or, in any case, none that human reason can identify). In this view, the attempt to defend positions about the ethical obligations of faculty is doomed from the start. This text could only reflect the opinions of its authors and will be accepted or rejected depending on the predilections of the individual reader. What professors decide to do in the classroom can only reflect the personal tastes and preferences of individual instructors. In defense of relativism, it can be argued both that there are in fact deep disagreements about ethical issues and also that there are no objectively verifiable means of resolving these disputes.

Although it is true that there is ethical disagreement, the conclusion of relativism is hasty. Lack of agreement does not imply that there are no correct answers. In any disagreement, some views may be right and some wrong; or the correct answer may not yet have been found. Objective science is itself characterized by disputes—from debates in physics about whether the quark is the smallest particle in the universe to debates in education over whether lecture or discussion is more effective in leading to student learning. Nobody thinks that because there is scientific disagreement, there are no right answers. So it is strange and unfortunate that the relativistic conclusion is drawn so readily in ethics.

Against relativism, it can also be argued that despite disagreement about some issues, there is widespread ethical agreement about fundamental matters. There are some moral values and principles which nobody disputes: For example, almost no one thinks it is okay to kill, torture, or rape an innocent child. Though there are debates about the morality of euthanasia and abortion, few question whether (in general) freedom of choice is a good and killing ought to be avoided. Ethical disagreements are usually about the implications and priority of these basic principles in particular situations. Thus, if relativism depends upon moral disagreement, it is on shaky ground (Rachels, 2003).

Ethicists such as Rachels have pointed out that few would wish to accept the implications of ethical relativism. To be consistent, a relativist would have to refrain from raising a moral objection to any conduct, something that is difficult for any human being to do. We live in relationships with others and have views about the conduct appropriate to society. We expect and demand that others live according to norms of mutual respect. When norms are trespassed, individuals argue with and protest those who break them. Such criticism implies that we believe some actions are wrong and others are obligatory and right. While many academics would argue for tolerance of a wide range of student and professorial behaviors, it is safe to say that most would object to some forms of conduct by their students and colleagues. For example, a relativist-leaning academic might object to harassing phone calls or physical assault by students, an action which betrays a belief in and commitment to objectively valid ethical norms. People in general, and academics in particular, cannot help but believe that there are better and worse ways of acting. Almost nobody is a sincere and consistent relativist.

One of the most common inconsistencies of relativism occurs when relativists argue for toleration. The argument goes that because there are no objectively valid truths in ethics we should all tolerate each other's actions. Yet this argument itself makes an ethical claim—that we should not attempt to force unproven ethical claims on others. Although this seems like a plausible moral principle, the relativists' assertion of this principle contradicts their conclusion. Alternatively, if this principle of toleration is a norm warranting ethical observance, then may not other moral principles be valid as well? Indeed, the value of toleration asserted by most relativists seems to presuppose that human freedom and human life are of general value and should be allowed to flourish. But if these are valued, then one is committed to a whole range of ethical principles which are conducive to human freedom and well-being.

That relativism is difficult to consistently maintain does not prove that there are objectively valid ethical principles. However, the unavoidable tendency to justify our actions by appealing to moral truth gives reason to inquire into ethical argument. If we can find norms of conduct which are rationally defensible and to which objections can be answered, there is good reason for thinking these norms are objectively valid. Thus, we will proceed with the assumption that our predisposition to justify our actions and ask for justification of others is sensible in both academics and other areas.

Personal Integrity, Conscience, and Ethics

We have argued for an ethics of teaching in part on the basis that individuals believe they have obligations (or, as it is sometimes put, individuals have consciences). Some would argue that ethics should be understood largely as a matter of personal integrity, in acting according to those norms which we are already committed to in principle. To avoid hypocrisy and live sincerely by those principles that we believe correct would appear to be a basic obligation. One might argue that if an individual did not believe in and was not committed to ethical principles, there is little point in recommending observance of such principles. However, taken to its logical conclusion this line of thought implies that ethical argument has little role to play in determining conduct, and therefore that it would be pointless to recommend ethical principles.

Though individual conscience plays an important role in ethical matters, it is not itself a completely reliable response to ethical issues. Individuals can be conscientiously convinced of mistaken principles: They may believe in overly harsh or overly lenient punishment. In such cases, ethical argument may help to correct and clarify individual views. Although individual consciences are not easily overturned, they may at times be changed after examination of the issues. Individuals may also be uncertain which of several principles to act on. In such cases ethical argument may help individuals make up their minds about the implications of their own ethical positions. Ethical argument may help to confirm that the conscience is right in a given situation. For all of these reasons, professors can benefit from consulting ethical reasoning as well as their own consciences. Although we can expect that individuals will generally act according to their own conscientious beliefs (and no ethical argument would work very well if it conflicted with consciences or failed to be incorporated into the ethical commitments of individuals), the current principles of professors cannot be assumed to be completely correct and adequate responses to ethical issues.

Expertise, Technique, Objectivity, and Teaching Ethics

A different kind of objection to the project of developing an ethic for university professors holds that while there are indeed better and worse ways for teachers to do things, such issues are matters of technique. In this view, the correct method for teaching should be answered by scientific research into the most effective forms of pedagogy, not by ethical argument and abstract moral principles. Instructors should employ those means which have been objectively shown to be most successful. For example, what mix of lecture and discussion is best would seem to be an empirical question; the same applies to whether to grade on a curve or fixed scale, whether to use essay or multiple-choice testing, or whether to have professors advocate for their beliefs or model neutrality. Many questions about how best to teach could potentially be answered by scientific inquiry.

   While a case can be made for each of these approaches, they beg the ethical questions involved by assuming that there is an objective understanding of "furthering education" which needs no defense and which can be unproblematically pursued by the most efficacious techniques. Education, we already saw, has several different purposes—individual development, the furthering of the common good, and inquiry into truth. Although there may be objective truth about the best way to foster the recollection of facts (say, by lecture and multiple-choice exams), this isn't the only purpose of education. Thus the fact that an educational goal is most effectively achieved through a particular means does not prove that this means should be employed. The use of this means may thwart other ethical goals or violate other ethical principles which are of equal or greater importance. To determine what principles are most important to pursue in the classroom, we will have to enter an ethical debate rather than a technical or scientific one. While an objective study of pedagogical effectiveness can help identify the best means to achieve some educational goals, it cannot tell us which goals are valuable and ought to be pursued.

In fact, some of the aims of education do not lend themselves to any objective measurement. Exactly what constitutes good critical thinking and individual creativity is itself a matter for ethical debate. Some have argued that education should foster good citizenship; although many educational researchers might agree, we would have to reflect on what good citizenship is before determining how to achieve it. What all this means is that the objective measurement of effective educational practice cannot resolve ethical questions about what should be taught—and it is even less able to address issues about what fairness toward and respectful treatment of students involves.

The scientistic view that all questions should be answered according to objectively measurable evidence has been defended by the philosophy of positivism. Positivists argue that only verifiable assertions are meaningful and rational. Ethical assertions about what ought to be done cannot be deduced from any set of facts and thus are unscientific.

While there is not room here for a detailed discussion of positivism, a couple points should be made in order to defend our ethical inquiry into teaching. First, positivism (like relativism) is internally contradictory. The principle that "no nonscientific statement has meaning" is itself a kind of metaphysical principle that cannot be verified but must be accepted or rejected on the basis of reason or intuition. Second, positivists (again, like relativists) tend to contradict themselves by making ethical prescriptions. For example, positivists have said that we should use the scientific method as the only rational method, and that it would be wrong to use other methods. But this is to assert a moral principle rather than a purely scientific truth. To be consistent, a positivist would have to refuse to make any ethical recommendations whatsoever. To consistently embrace positivism would mean to endorse a moral skepticism in which one doubted all moral obligations, an implausible conclusion.

Just as relativism gives up on ethical inquiry too quickly, a strictly empirical approach begs too many questions about ethics. In a sense, scientism gives up on the ability of reason to tell us anything about the ends of human existence as well as the means. An ethics of education, by contrast, must explore the ends of education as well as its means.

Cost-Effectiveness and Teaching Ethics

Of course, technical considerations about effective pedagogy are not the only factors which influence educational decisions. Professors are also influenced by and pressured to make teaching decisions according to financial efficiency. Courses are taught as large lectures to boost the production of student credit hours and increase university income. Other courses are taught online or in intensive night course meetings once a week to satisfy student demand and attract new students. In the classroom there is some pressure on instructors to inflate grades and graduate students. Financial incentives, as well as the pressure of student expectations, support this: Higher graduation rates and grades look good to school funders, keep and attract students, and result in appreciative alumni.

On the other hand, structuring classes so that students are likely to pass does not necessarily foster the spread of knowledge, individual development, or the good of the community. Thus professors rightly see it as an obligation to resist pressures to inflate grades, dumb down course material, and adopt teaching methods on the basis of financial considerations. In general, educators are obligated to teach to the best of their ability with available resources without regard to costs. Other things being equal, resources should not be wasted—professors should reduce paper and energy use when possible. However, within the limits of their budgets, academics ought not cut corners to save money if this would harm education. For example, if a professor thinks running off a lecture outline or review sheet is helpful for students, he or she ought to do it. Professors are responsible for wisely using their allocated resources while trying to teach, research, and serve the community as well as possible.

Perhaps the most important financial obligation of academics is not to waste their students' money. Students generally have minimal income and cost affects their access to and ability to succeed in college. Students each term delay purchasing texts or do not purchase them at all because of cost considerations. Sometimes professors list texts as required which are hardly used or for which there are less expensive alternatives. Professors should assign only those materials necessary for course completion and, when given a choice, should take into account affordability.

Academic Freedom and Teaching Ethics

The discussion of professorial obligations immediately raises the issue of academic freedom. Does the assertion of educator responsibilities not entail arguing for a reduction of academic freedom? The short answer is that the assertion of professorial obligations does not conflict with respect for academic freedom. To appreciate the connection between academic freedom and obligations, it is helpful to review the nature of and reasons for academic freedom.

Academic freedom involves a right held on the part of academics to conduct inquiry, both in research and in teaching, without fear of repercussion for the methods used or conclusions reached. It includes stipulations that academics are not to be fired for their ideological views and that they not be pressured to change their research or teaching methods. The institution of tenure, of course, helps to preserve academic freedom by allowing professors freedom to teach and inquire in their areas of study without fear of being let go if their work is viewed as wrongheaded, valueless, or dangerous. Not just tenured professors, but also tenure-track and adjunct faculty are given rights to design their own courses and pursue their own research agendas. Such instructors are not supposed to be let go for their beliefs and academic approaches, though they have less job security from year to year.

To some extent academic freedom can be simply viewed as an extension of the First Amendment right of free speech into the academic realm. In addition to forbidding the arrest and punishment of people for their speech, U.S. law has protected the rights of employees, especially public employees, to speak out on political issues outside their jobs without penalty on the job. The freedom to think and talk about controversial topics is central to living as a free individual and as a citizen in a democratic society.

However, academic freedom goes beyond normal rights of free speech and due process in employment. Academic freedom involves a right not just to engage in speech outside one's job without punishment by job loss, but autonomy in one's conduct of one's employment itself. Typically employees can be ordered to use particular methods and support particular ideas, and can be fired for the way in which they conduct their jobs and the types of ideas and conclusions they support during their work. Although certainly many employees in business and government are given autonomy to conduct their own projects as they see fit, academic freedom involves a more systematic protection than almost any other field. Academic freedom is unusual in the amount of autonomy that the worker is given to plan his or her own projects without guidelines or supervision.

Since the rights of academics go beyond the rights of other citizens and employees, the defense of academic freedom must be understood in terms of its benefit to society rather than as any kind of natural or basic human right. The argument for academic freedom in particular is similar to John Stuart Mill's utilitarian argument for freedom of speech: The benefits of allowing free inquiry as opposed to its repression outweigh any harms that result from the problematic use of the right. Free inquiry allows for a "marketplace of ideas," in which the truth is most likely to emerge. The attempt to suppress bad ideas may result in the suppression of unpopular beliefs which turn out to be true. Examples abound in which beliefs which were formerly repressed are now widely accepted and valued: early proponents of the heliocentric view of the universe, Darwinian evolution, and most of the world's religious beliefs faced initial persecution. Attempts to ban or stifle foolish, bad, or harmful speech risk the suppression of new ideas and emerging knowledge. On the other hand, allowing all ideas to be aired and tested should allow bad ideas to be rejected. Even in those cases in which current beliefs are already correct and alternative views misguided, Mill argues that allowing free speech is valuable. It forces the true beliefs—for example, those in democracy and human rights—to be defended, leading to a better understanding of them. Furthermore, allowing wrongheaded views to be publicly expressed makes it more likely that they can be refuted and their adherents won over to the truth (Mill, 1859/1989).

Mill's arguments appear to apply even more centrally to academic freedom than to liberty in ordinary public speech. The academy is charged with being the locus for the discovery of truth and the development of knowledge. Therefore, insofar as the freedom to formulate, express, and criticize views is necessary to the advancement of knowledge, it is critical that this exist for academic researchers. Indeed, the very nature of inquiry into the truth would seem to require freedom. The scientific testing of beliefs requires that they be expressed publicly and be open to criticism.

While this argument makes a decisive case for academic freedom in research, it isn't as clear that it applies to classroom teaching. The classroom is not generally where new knowledge is discovered. Professors are generally concerned with teaching what is already known; their goal in the classroom is not to advance knowledge, but to facilitate student learning. Thus freedom of inquiry in the classroom promises little benefit in terms of socially advantageous discoveries. At the same time, the risks of allowing academic freedom in teaching seem relatively great. The freedom to write articles and books on most any topic seems relatively harmless, as they only can gain influence insofar as people choose to read and accept them. By contrast, the freedom to teach anything to classrooms (of usually young and relatively uninformed thinkers who may be susceptible to manipulation and for whom the professor is an authority) appears fraught with risk. Students may be influenced to accept foolish or even dangerous ideas or may have their education curtailed by the teaching of unimportant material in an ineffective manner.

Yet academic freedom in the classroom does facilitate the process of inquiry. The classroom is a place in which professors try out new theories and avenues of inquiry. Professors frequently discuss and apply ideas in the classroom before they arrange them for publication to the wider academic community. Faculty are continually urged to connect their teaching and research roles. While the effective pursuit of one goal inevitably conflicts with the other, frequently material discussed in teaching furthers research—and that research in turn enlivens the classroom. Thus freedom to introduce new and unpopular ideas in the classroom contributes to progress in the social quest of knowledge.

However, the primary argument for academic freedom in the class-room is somewhat different. As Mill argues, freedom of inquiry con-tributes not only to the advance of knowledge but also to the development of mature, responsible, and reflective individuals (Mill, 1859/1989). While a great deal of this development is for the individual who is allowed to experiment with new ideas, there is also development on the part of the audience that encounters new ideas. In the university, it is this development of the audience that is the main argument for aca-demic freedom in the classroom. Students, as well as instructors, are ben-eficiaries of the instructor's freedom to introduce unpopular and unconventional ideas and teaching methods in the classroom.

Given this defense of academic freedom as well as its widespread recognition in law and university policy, the question arises whether it makes sense to speak of professorial obligations. After all, if there is a right to academic freedom, this must include a right to do wrong (Gewirth, 1990). A right which is conditional upon its good use is no real right. Academic freedom means allowing professors to say and do things in the classroom that are thought mistaken by interested observers—including students, colleagues, administrators, parents, funders, and taxpayers. Although faculty must be allowed to teach in ways which are flawed, this is compatible with recognizing that faculty have an obligation to teach well and to fulfill various ethical obligations in their teaching.

First, there are limits to academic freedom. The right of free inquiry stops when it conflicts with the rights of others. Thus, the freedom to experiment in the classroom stops at the point where it infringes on the rights of students. Thus, academic freedom does not include a right to abuse or discriminate against students. Although educators are free to employ various methods, they must still meet with their classes and grade students—otherwise faculty fall below the minimum that can be legally expected. Many ethical dilemmas in the classroom will be about the ques-tion of when professors do in fact violate student rights.

Second, we have seen that faculty have obligations beyond the duty to treat students decently. To say that professors have a right to teach in a flawed manner does not mean that there is no obligation to teach responsibly and effectively. As with any right, although we are allowed to misuse it, we ought not misuse it. Freedom of speech gives one the right to defend the idea that the earth is flat, to tell lies, and to harp about trivial matters, but one ought not do so. Similarly, academic freedom ought to be used well, even though it involves a right to be mistaken. Many of the ethical obligations discussed in this book will be things that professors cannot legally be required to do without violating academic freedom, but which nonetheless they ought to do.

Not only is the right of academic freedom compatible with professorial obligations, but we argued earlier that it implies duties. The argument that rights imply duties is common. However, the duties that are most directly implied by rights are the duties of other individuals to the holder of the rights. If one has a right to academic freedom, others have an obligation not to interfere with this right. However, as Alan Gewirth (1990) argues, the person who acquires rights by taking on a particular role also acquires the duties of that role. For example, military officers have the right to command but also have responsibilities that go along with the privileges of that office. Likewise, academics, by taking on the role of the professor—for which they are given freedom of inquiry, inside and outside the classroom—have a responsibility to use this freedom to attempt to further knowledge, benefit society, and contribute to the growth of students—those duties already discussed. The university and the society grant this right to the professor in exchange for the professor using it to fulfill this obligation. Although a professor does not promise to teach specific types of material in specific types of ways, he or she does promise to teach in order to satisfy academic aims. Because others generally cannot pressure academics to meet these duties without violating academic freedom, it devolves to educators themselves to make themselves aware of and carry out their obligations.

Conclusion

Ethical reflection on the role of a faculty member, the purpose of education, and the nature of interpersonal morality reveal several forms of obligations for faculty members. This discussion suggests the following preliminary list to guide faculty in their teaching of students:

1) Professors should foster knowledge and inquiry by:
   • Preparing and conducting courses in a way which facilitates learning
   • Remaining truthful and avoiding deception in the presentation of material
   • Remaining committed to the ideals of critical inquiry into the truth

2) Professors should contribute to student development by:
   • Fostering the development of independent reflection
   • Not interfering with the freedom of student inquiry

3) Professors should treat students with respect, including refraining from harming, abusing, or denigrating students.

4) Professors should attempt to foster student well-being by:
   • Helping students with questions and problems related to or apparent in coursework
   • Designing courses and giving academic advice which fosters students' legitimate interests

5) Professors should treat students equitably in the provision and grading of courses by:
   • Not discriminating against students because of group membership
   • Applying rules consistently and fairly, treating like cases alike and different cases differently

6) Professors should contribute to social utility by:
   • Teaching students material that is likely to foster social well-being
   • Helping students develop as citizens of a democratic society

2

Teaching Controversy: Advocacy, Indoctrination, and Neutrality in the Classroom

The greatest recent public fervor over the conduct of professors has revolved around faculty politics. Professors have come under fire for making critical statements about the U.S. government and its war on terrorism, most famously in Ward Churchill's remarks comparing some 9/11 victims to "little Eichmanns." Such cases were referenced repeatedly as conservatives attempted to alert the public that university faculty possess ideologies different from those of the government and most Americans. Right-wing pundits called for the disciplining and dismissal of unpatriotic faculty and their replacement with intellectuals more loyal to the American government and possessing values and ideologies more closely matching those of the increasingly conservative American public.

Much of the concern over the politics of the professorate is that as educators they are poised to use the classroom to promote their political views. Proposals have emerged for ensuring a "Students' Bill of Rights," which would minimize faculty's ability to advocate for moral, political, and religious views in the classroom. These proposals would guarantee students:

> The right to expect that their academic freedom will not be infringed upon by instructors who create a hostile environment toward their political or religious beliefs, or who introduce controversial matter into the classroom or course work that is substantially unrelated to the subject of study. (Tennessee Senate Bill 1117, 2005)

The assessment of proposed legislation is not our main interest here. Briefly, the Students' Bill of Rights should be defeated, because such external regulation is unnecessary and would hinder rather than further students' academic freedom. The legislation would employ ambiguous terminology—a "hostile [intellectual] environment," "controversial matter," and "substantially unrelated"—which invites overly broad interpretation and discriminatory use. It would likely be used only to silence professors with unpopular views—not professors who promote nationalist political agendas. Such laws would discourage professors from bringing up controversial issues, thus limiting education: an unusually good example of a chilling effect. Furthermore, the principle that professors should not introduce controversial, unrelated material into the classroom has long been a principle of the American Association of University Professors (AAUP) and is also a requirement stipulated in many university teaching contracts. The formulation of a new student right would make it easier for students to bring costly lawsuits for grievances which can be dealt with in academia's internal complaints processes.

While these concerns are sufficient to oppose new laws curtailing academic freedom, underlying this debate is a fundamental ethical question for professors: When is it ethical for faculty to *advocate* for their own beliefs and values in the classroom, attempting to persuade students to adopt what the professor takes to be good moral, political, and religious views? Some argue that all classroom advocacy violates professorial obligations and amounts to unethical and educationally harmful *indoctrination*. Critics of professorial advocacy argue that classroom material should be presented in a *neutral* manner which does not endorse particular views or attempt to persuade students of their correctness. We will take a second approach, arguing that although advocacy has risks and indoctrination must be avoided, instructors can use the classroom to promote some beliefs and values.

Note that in answering this question, it is not enough to simply assert that professors' academic freedom gives them a *right* to advocate any view that they wish. The question remains whether one *ought* to do this. As we argued in Chapter 1, rights include a right to do some wrong, but one should not use one's rights to do wrong.

Defining Advocacy

In order to determine its ethical status, we need a definition of advocacy. The core meaning of professorial advocacy under dispute is the attempt to influence students to accept the professor's own views as the truth. Classroom advocacy involves professors not simply providing alternative positions for student consideration, but rather attempting to cultivate correct student conclusions about class material—particularly controversial moral, political, and religious issues.

Some have argued that a necessary part of classroom advocacy is that professors explicitly identify their own views (Markie, 1996). The paradigm case of a classroom advocate may be the individual who declares himself or herself to be a partisan of a particular view: a Marxist, a conservative, feminist, and so on. A literal reading of "advocacy" implies a role as public spokesperson.

However, explicit endorsement of a view is not a necessary feature of classroom advocacy. What is considered problematic about one stating one's own view in a classroom is that such a statement might pressure or otherwise influence students to adopt this view as well. On the other hand, professors who wish to influence their students in the classroom are probably more likely to succeed if they do not explicitly announce their own beliefs or intentions. If a professor announces that she takes a particular perspective, this is likely to trigger skepticism and defensiveness on the part of students. However, if the same professor discusses features of contemporary society and makes critical comments which stem from and point toward Marxist, conservative, or feminist conclusions, students may be more receptive to the ideas. Such an attempt to influence students to accept one's conclusions is still a form of advocacy regardless of how subtle and covert the method. It is the intent and active effort to persuade, not the announcing of one's position, that defines advocacy.

The Initial Case for Advocacy in Education

So to what extent should professors advocate or remain neutral? The initial case for advocacy appears plain. Teaching involves the sharing of knowledge with students. As certified experts in their fields, professors are supposed to fill in gaps in student understanding. Certainly, professors may assert facts to be true. We don't expect mathematicians to say "according to an influential theory of geometry, the sum of the angles of a triangle are 180 degrees" or geologists to say "according to one paradigm, the earth is billions of years old." For the sake of accuracy in representing the state of their disciplines, as well as for the sake of avoiding long and awkward qualifications, teachers simply state such things to be the case. Perhaps professors do well to explain the arguments and evidence for such facts. However, at some point explanations of how information is known becomes cumbersome and it is necessary to move on without complete arguments. Professors rightly hope that their students will *believe* basic facts about the universe to be true. Indeed, the most literal interpretation of the word "professor" indicates a person who affirms or declares certain things to be the case.

If professors can advocate for the truth of basic facts, should they not be able to advocate for other beliefs and values too? Are professors of the humanities and social sciences not in a position to advocate for their conclusions regarding morality, religion, and politics? If professors have thought through controversial issues such as abortion, euthanasia, same sex marriage, and the Iraq War, should they not present their conclusions openly and try to get students to accept their well-reasoned positions as correct? As Mike Martin (1997) puts it, faculty have a "truth-responsibility to advance knowledge" and this "truth-responsibility invites advocacy" (p. 20).

Indeed, many have wondered whether it is even possible to avoid advocacy and be neutral in teaching. Many concur with Robert Paul Wolff (1994) that advocacy is inevitable in education and neutrality is a myth. If we are going to consider the ethical obligations of professors with regard to refraining from promoting their views in the classroom, we must first examine the extent to which the latter is even a feasible goal.

Necessary and Avoidable Advocacy

It is impossible to avoid advocacy in some senses. If advocacy is defined in terms of effectively promoting particular values, then all teaching does this. For unless teaching is totally ineffective—and surely the most jaded among us would not say this—it will provide students with some abilities and knowledge which influence their opportunities for action. Teaching will have furthered some causes at the expense of others. For example, if one teaches critical thinking skills to a class that is mostly Republican, one may help Republicans more effectively pursue their own values. Likewise, if one teaches soldiers, nursing students, or business students, one effectively promotes some values over others.

As Holmes (1973) argues, this means that neutrality is impossible if it is to mean neutrality of *outcomes*. If there is a form of neutrality that would even be possible for instructors to implement, it would have to a neutrality of *intention* or intended outcomes. Perhaps instructors could refrain from encouraging particular values even though, as a matter of fact, their classes will have some moral influence.

However, even intending strict neutrality would be infeasible, or at least absurdly ineffectual. Education, by definition, intends to promote the values of knowledge, truthfulness, critical thinking, disciplined study, intellectual honesty, and logical consistency (Martin, 1997; Simon, 1994). A commitment to principles and virtues of intellectual inquiry distinguishes education from other processes of public influence, such as entertainment or propaganda. Even the argument that education should be neutral presupposes that teachers should promote the value of student autonomy. Insofar as autonomous decision-making is not to be the mere statement of preferences, autonomy itself requires virtues such as critical thinking and broad-mindedness.

An impartial learning environment that allows all students to develop and express their views also requires the general observance of other principles and values such as tolerance, civility, and mutual respect. To the extent that any of these values are lacking, it is educationally necessary that teachers advocate them in the classroom.

It could be objected that professors need only promote broad-minded, independent, rational, and civil inquiry in their courses, but need not try to cultivate permanent student adoption of these values. But surely this is too narrow a view of the goal of education. Education ought to seek to influence students to develop and retain the habits and values of inquiry. Professors who failed to advocate for educational values would shirk their duties.

In addition to the aims of education, the very process of organizing and directing a course requires that teachers make choices based upon values, thereby actively promoting them (Martin, 1997; Myers & Tronto,

1998). Educators must select course topics and texts, and allocate class time for each. Although a course can cover a range of issues and perspectives, a finite semester requires some selectivity. Some topics and texts have to be rejected as comparatively unimportant. It could be argued that professors should make curricular and course planning decisions according to purely objective standards, such as factual accuracy, logical consistency, and appropriate inference from evidence. But these criteria are almost certainly insufficient to determine course content. Such decisions involve a judgment about the quality of various works, the social importance of the issues they discuss, the plausibility of competing theories, and the importance of a diversity of perspectives (such as the inclusion of marginalized, minority perspectives). Even objective issues such as factual accuracy and logical consistency must be given evaluative weights, not themselves purely objectively derived, in order to rank various texts and topics. Professorial decisions are inevitably based upon values.

However, it would be hasty to conclude that because a good deal of advocacy is inevitable, professors should go ahead and advocate for their views about *any and all* matters. Instead, one might concur with Holmes (1973) that advocacy is appropriate insofar as it is educationally necessary, while still holding that other forms of advocacy should be avoided. Thus advocacy of critical, rigorous, and evidentially based inquiry (and the corresponding virtues of tolerance and civility) should be fostered. Professors should design courses in light of their reasonable interpretations of the standards of their disciplines. Such forms of advocacy are necessary if education is to happen at all. However, other advocacy is not educationally necessary. Professors need not take stands on controversial moral and political issues in order for education to occur. They could instead introduce a range of ideas about an issue consistent with disciplinary standards without attempting to persuade students of the rightness of one view.

Yet it could be argued that the difficulties of avoiding advocacy apply even, or perhaps especially, to controversial issues. If education is to bring up socially relevant issues, then professors will possess views on the issues discussed in class. It will be difficult for educators to refrain from interjecting their own strongly held views. Even if professors avoid giving lectures about the right answer to a particular question, they are likely to subtly indicate their approval of ideas through vocal tone and body language. One argues more eloquently and passionately for ideas which one believes. Even when professors seek to be Socratic, asking questions of students but not providing answers, they are likely to find themselves asking harder questions of those with whom they disagree. Samuel Calhoun (1996) recounts his attempt to remain neutral while teaching a class on the morality and politics of abortion, despite possessing strong personal views on the issue. He found himself unable to refrain from supporting his own side of this debate more forcefully and questioning it less rigorously than the opposing side. It would seem that it is very difficult for a professor to avoid advocacy of any position about which he or she cares deeply. Taken to its logical conclusion, the goal of avoiding advocacy would have the absurd implication that professors should only teach courses on material about which they are disinterested, and therefore probably relatively disengaged and uninformed.

While it is probably impossible to strictly refrain from exhibiting any ideological favoritism, this does not fully resolve the question of advocacy. It is still possible for professors to intentionally minimize advocacy on matters not educationally necessary. Instructors can attain degrees of success in refraining from revealing their own views and pressuring students to accept their conclusions. Teaching may be no different from other social roles which require impartiality, like those of judges and juries. Although it is inevitable for prior views to affect how one does one's job, it is possible to maintain neutrality as a goal. There has probably never been a professor who attained complete neutrality in the classroom, but some strive to create an environment in which a range of views are discussed in a balanced and unbiased manner.

Indeed many professors—having engaged in Socratic questioning, devil's advocacy, or the presentation of pro and con arguments on more than one side of an issue—have had frustrated students ask what the professor's actual views are. Michael Bérubé (1996) cites his experience of having students surprised to discover his actual political views upon reading about his work outside of the classroom. On the other hand, educators as well as students sometimes wonder if they have gone too far in pushing for their own views in the classroom. Such experiences imply that professors are able to choose degrees of advocacy in their teaching. These alternative goals and methods require moral and practical evaluation.

The Case Against Advocacy

There are several arguments against unnecessary classroom advocacy and for professorial neutrality. One argument holds that there can be no knowledge regarding values. This claim has been defended by logical positivists and ethical relativists, who argue that there are no objective criteria for moral, political, or religious truth; assertions about these matters can only be statements of the opinions, preferences, and feelings of the professor. Since professors are supposed to impart knowledge and not opinions and preferences, assertions regarding at least evaluative claims can be argued to have no place in teaching. Max Weber famously endorsed this fact/value dichotomy, using it to support a policy of value-free education (Weaver, 1998).

We discussed in the first chapter that there are reasons to doubt positivism and relativism as moral theories. The contradictory and counter-intuitive implications of relativism are apparent in arguments such as Weber's. Weber suggests that it would be *wrong* to teach values, given the impossibility of ethical knowledge. In making this argument, however, Weber asserts an ethical principle as objectively valid and defends it with reasons, contradicting his own relativism.

Yet there is a stronger form of this objection which does not rest on a categorical rejection of validity in ethics. This form holds that there are no ethical *experts*; although there may be moral truths, professorial research gives no particular ability to discern them. Professors' fields of expertise may give them insight into facts and the structure of reasoning, including perhaps the structure of arguments in ethics. However, since various professors come down on different sides of contested issues, one might conclude that there is reasonable disagreement about these issues and that none of the sides knows their own view to be correct. If so, professors ought not present their own views as if they were knowledge. This fallibilistic case against advocacy does not presuppose that there are no moral, political, and religious truths. It only states that none of us knows these truths with such certainty that we are justified in presenting our views to others as knowledge.

The argument that a professor's moral and political views lack certainty is insufficient in itself to prove that these views shouldn't be advocated.

After all, the professor's views may be relatively well reasoned and may help students to reach better conclusions. If it were wrong to make assertions about uncertain moral, political, and religious matters, then libraries are filled with the work of unethical charlatans. The case against advocacy ultimately rests on additional arguments specific to the professional role of the professor and the institutional setting of the classroom.

Elias Baumgarten (1982) has argued that educators should recognize the fallibility of their disciplines and should view instruction as the mutual pursuit of knowledge rather than its dissemination by an authority: "University teachers have a social obligation to help other citizens . . . formulate reasoned principles for themselves" (p. 282). In light of this goal, Baumgarten argues that education, especially in the humanities, should be Socratic. In this model, professors serve as facilitators who encourage students to critically question ideas and consider alternative perspectives. According to Baumgarten, professorial declarations that give the best answers not only are unnecessary but also interfere with the educational mission of fostering independent, critical reflection:

> For an instructor to present one position as being the "strongest" shortcuts the process of questioning that is the essence of humanistic study; and it may deprive students of the creative anguish that comes with having to think through an issue and come to a conclusion purely by assessing opposing arguments, not knowing in advance what the "correct" position is supposed to be. (pp. 290–291)

Providing the tools for free agency rather than training students how to live their lives has been central to the definition of a "liberal" education, the provision of which is an explicit goal of most universities in the United States. If educators share ideas and concepts with students, but allow students to reach their own conclusions, individual autonomy is preserved.

One might question whether and why the promotion of autonomy is the fundamental value in education. Isn't it more important that a student reach the *right* conclusions and become a *good* person than she reach her *own* conclusions and become her own person? Liberal political philosophy and educational theory has plausibly argued that individual liberty trumps social utility (Dworkin, 1977; Rawls, 1971). If we could achieve brilliant and well-behaved students through brainwashing them or secretly implanting mind-control devices, we ought not to do it. This is in part because the implanted views could be wrong and thus do more harm than the encouragement of individual thinking. The life of a democratic society depends on citizens being able to raise questions and generate ideas without accepting the authoritative views of elites. If universities are to educate citizens and make them prepared for democratic participation, their education should ask them to develop their own reasoned views in response to issues. If their professors tell them what to think about difficult issues, they will be not be pushed to think them through for themselves, and will not have experience exercising independent reasoning and judgment when they become active in civil society and politics. We maintain that an autonomous citizenry is necessary for democracy.

Autonomy also has intrinsic value. Our resistance to programming individuals, even to make them happy and effective members of society, implies that autonomy is valuable for its own sake. The free choice of other goods—such as knowledge, pleasure, or faith—enhances their value. A valuable life must be one of one's own choosing. Although presumably individuals can lead autonomous lives without a higher education, one function of postsecondary study is to enable independence in thought and action.

While we agree with Baumgarten (1982) that professors ought to encourage rather than interfere with student autonomy, we disagree with the suggestion that professorial advocacy is incompatible with student freedom of thought. The attempt to persuade does not constitute coercion. If it did, our freedom would be robbed every time we attended a speech or read an essay. It is difficult to force anyone to believe anything, both because human minds have a way of reaching their own conclusions and because compliance in belief cannot be verified and enforced. Thus, professorial advocacy of views may leave students free to decide whether to be persuaded. Indeed, insofar as advocacy presents new ideas to the audience to consider, it would seem to enhance the autonomy of listeners (Benjamin, 1996).

The validity of the autonomy argument for neutrality ultimately rests on yet another argument: that the professor's power in the classroom makes advocacy a form of illegitimate *indoctrination*. Professors' power stems from at least two different types of authority. One is the authority of expertise conferred on the professor by their social role, title, knowledge, and experience. Students are encouraged to trust their professors' expertise. Furthermore, college students tend to be young and inexperienced, their views relatively unformed and uninformed. As a result, students are susceptible to intellectual influence. A class in literature, history, politics, or philosophy may be the students' first and only opportunity to hear from an expert on the subject. Compared to students and their usual conversational partners, professors tend to have more intellectual background and rhetorical skill. College students are on the whole unprepared to dispute their professor's assertions. Charismatic or even moderately articulate faculty, with access to youth in their formative stage for three hours a week, have an opportunity to influence a generation.

Professors also have the power and institutional authority to grade students. This allows professors to compel attendance, regulate discussion, and evaluate student work. When classroom attendance is required to receive a passing grade, teachers have a captive audience. In discussion and writing assignments, students may feel pressure to accept or even mimic their professor's views instead of questioning them. Insofar as vigorous dissent by students is risky, professorial advocacy is likely to be unchallenged—compounding its power. In these ways, a professor's status is very different from that of a visiting lecturer, who cannot compel attendance or punish dissent.

Of course, many professors will object that they have difficulty getting their students to attend class regularly much less unquestioningly absorb and mimic every word they say. Even when students do mimic professors' views, it is questionable to what degree this results in a genuine loss of autonomy. Many professors have received student papers which take little note of the professor's view. Other papers parrot what the student takes to be the instructor's view but do so insincerely. Such insincerity, while not ideal, also attests to the limits in faculty's ability to actually influence students. It could be argued that students do not need to be free to exercise their freedom of speech and dissent *in class* when they are free to develop their own ideas in the large portion of their lives spent outside of the classroom.

However, if professorial advocacy serves to limit students' expression of their own views in the classroom and in coursework, this is an educational and ethical problem. Although time spent in class is only a fraction of students' lives, this time is supposed to allow them intense and independent reflection on intellectual issues. Although a student is always free to silently explore his or her personal response to course content, to be able to actively speak and write about one's ideas and get civil feedback from others is an important way to develop one's views. In Chapter 1, we discussed the reasons for professorial academic freedom in the classroom, arguing that class discussion is an important venue for testing ideas. The same arguments indicate a need for student academic freedom. In addition to favoring academic freedom for the speaker's benefit, we should also recall that academic freedom benefits listeners. This goes for the academic freedom of students as well as professors. Students can and ideally should benefit from the comments and questions of their classmates. If professorial advocacy silences opposition in the classroom, then students lose academic freedom. Legal opinion has seconded these ethical arguments; courts have concluded that students, as well as faculty, have the right to academic freedom (*Rosenberger v. Rector and Visitors of the University of Virginia*, 1995). While advocacy is supported by the faculty's right of academic freedom, it is potentially at odds with that of students.

The Nature of Indoctrination

So far the proposal is that classroom advocacy, by using power to influence student decisions, is a form of indoctrination that violates students' academic freedom and harms their education. However, while it is almost universally agreed that indoctrination is bad and to be avoided, it is important to define exactly what counts as indoctrination. Educational theorists have devoted considerable energy to defining indoctrination and describing its deviation from genuine education. Analyses of the concept agree that not all influence is indoctrination (Snook, 1972). If professors use their power to influence students to conclude that $2 + 2 = 4$ or to value logic, theory, art, and literature, we do not think this is a problem. Indeed, professors are hired in part to influence students in such directions. We hope that they will use their position, knowledge, and skills to make a difference in students' lives.

It could be argued that advocacy becomes indoctrination only when it attempts to influence students on controversial matters regarding politics, morality, and religion. When uncontroversial goods and truths are promoted, few decry this use of professorial influence. It is professors' promotion of their views on contested social issues that causes worries about the abuse of authority and indoctrination.

Nonetheless, it is not clear what is wrong with influencing students on controversial matters. Do individuals have a right not to be influenced on matters of importance? This argument assumes a conception of autonomy in which judgments are ideally formed independently of all external, or at least institutional, influence. But this is an impossible and mistaken conception of autonomy. Autonomous judgments are always influenced by the views of others. Almost all ideas people have are things that they have heard or read somewhere else. Furthermore, the greatest influences possess power either because of social role (e.g., parent, preacher, government official, star athlete, entertainer) or expertise (e.g., author, television commentator). One may regret that influence by some of these sources is as great as it is. However, it would be pernicious to argue that all influence by sources with social power should be abolished, such that students should reach their own conclusions free from any consultation of experts or authorities. Nor is it clear why influence by professors is uniquely problematic.

In order to get at what seems problematic in the use of power to influence, we need to return to more precise attempts to define "indoctrination." Writers on the subject of indoctrination have concluded that indoctrination involves nonrational persuasion (Snook, 1972). Indoctrination, unlike the attempt to persuade through reasoned argument, attempts to get individuals to accept beliefs as true without regard to reasons or evidence. Indoctrination can be identified by the *intention* of a speaker to cultivate acceptance of a belief *resistant to rational reflection or criticism*. Of course, intentions can be difficult to discern, but individuals can sometimes recognize in themselves and others the intention to instill beliefs fixedly. For a professor to attempt this is to violate his or her duty to respect students as autonomous individuals.

Indoctrination can also be defined and identified by the *methods* of persuasion employed. Indoctrination uses nonrational means to get an audience to believe the speaker's assertions. There are several forms of irrational persuasion which constitute indoctrination. Irrational means include, obviously, lying—making up facts to persuade students to adopt a particular view is unethical, and disrespects the listener as a rational agent. In addition to direct lies, however, other forms of distortion also constitute deception and interfere with rational understanding of an issue. Distortion can involve intentional ambiguity or a refusal to acknowledge relevant objections or alternatives. Professors should attempt to indicate the range of scholarly debate about a topic, even if they are not neutral about where the truth ultimately lies. Defining what counts as a "fair and balanced" presentation of material is notoriously difficult. Needless to say, professors need not present every conceivable perspective regarding topics under inquiry. Time and pedagogical effectiveness require some simplification and bracketing in lecture and discussion. A general policy is that professors should present the arguments and information that a reasonable, informed party would view relevant to a discussion in these circumstances. What amount and type of material is relevant depends on the level of the course and how much course time is allotted to the topic. The central point is that if a view is asserted dogmatically as unproblematic and certain when there are important objections, this is deceptive and distorting.

Open and rational inquiry is also thwarted if educators use their authority to silence debate. The spirit of inquiry and rational persuasion requires that questions are allowed to be voiced. Professors ought not use the authority of their voice or the threat of sanctions to prevent a reasonable amount of discussion, even if such discussion is critical of what the professor takes to be the correct view. Professors may gently correct or question student assertions without denying academic freedom or slipping into indoctrination. Professors also can and should sometimes cut off discussion due to time constraints or when student comments become uncivil, tangential, or otherwise unhelpful. But if debate is silenced entirely and discussion prevented in order to preserve the view the professor advocates, then lecture becomes propagandistic indoctrination.

The use of certain forms of irrational persuasion also constitutes indoctrination. For example, the logical fallacy called appeal to authority—in which listeners are urged to accept a conclusion simply because a revered source (the Bible, Thomas Jefferson, or Milton Friedman) states that it is true—can be persuasive, but is mistaken. Emotional speech can also be used to persuade without argument. We are familiar with the tactics of demagogues who use fear, doubt, anger, and confusion to get an audience to be receptive to their ideologies and policies. Though professors have smaller audiences than dictators, they too can be guilty of such appeals. This is not to say that all emotional appeal must be avoided. This is both impossible to achieve and counterproductive to attempt. All effective rhetoric makes some use of affect to capture and maintain the audience's interest. Clearly instructors should display and inspire concern and enthusiasm regarding issues discussed in class. Use of emotional speech crosses into indoctrination when it is relied on to convince students to accept a controversial proposal without giving them reasons for doing so. Emotional appeal should only accompany good reasons and not be substituted for them.

On this account, most classroom advocacy is not indoctrination. A professor endorsing a view or attempting to illustrate its virtues need not involve coercion, silencing of debate, or irrational appeals. Professors who advocate for positions can and should give reasons and evidence for the views defended, rather than asserting positions to be accepted by students as articles of faith. Faculty also should have a clear policy that respectfully disputing the professor's arguments in class discussion and writing is encouraged and will not incur punishment. It is possible, indeed common, for professors to invite objections and counterarguments to the views they defend.

Although not all advocacy is indoctrination, professors should be aware that some advocacy is indoctrination. When professors command or beg a class to accept their views, silence or punish students with dissenting views, cut off debate on a topic after making a political barb, or ridicule opposing arguments while failing to note any potential shortcoming of their own views, faculty are engaged in indoctrination and have exceeded ethical limits in their advocacy.

Other Reasons for Neutrality

To this point, we have argued that advocacy is only wrong when it takes the form of indoctrination. While ruling out some bad practices, this would still allow considerable advocacy. Some might be suspicious that this overreaches professors' roles. It could be argued that professors are bound by explicit contract with their institutions and by implicit contract with students to teach courses according to catalogue descriptions. Course descriptions normally mention that a class will cover issues, theories and facts relating to a particular subject: 19th century literature, African American history, environmental biology, organic chemistry, etc. They rarely state that the course will involve advocacy for a particular view. Perhaps some courses, which focus on a particular theory (Marxism, feminism, or conservatism), imply that the theory will be advocated as true, or at least valuable. However, most course descriptions do not suggest advocacy of a particular viewpoint. In such courses, professorial advocacy could be argued to violate the terms of one's promises to the institution and students.

However, it would be a mistake to rule out advocacy simply because it is not mentioned in the catalogue or syllabus. It is not possible to list every topic that will be covered or every pedagogical method that will be employed. Professors may use maps, handouts, discussion groups, or quizzes, even if students were not forewarned upon entry into the course. Any methods relevant to the subject matter of the course may be employed. Furthermore, advocacy frequently *is* relevant to course topics. In courses dealing with history, politics, ethics, and sociological forces, *controversial* issues arise. Moral judgments about things such as slavery, war, abortion, discrimination, and economic policies will be relevant to these discussions. Insofar as the professor has informed and well-reasoned views on such issues, it follows that these are germane as well. Introduction of these views, as with the implementation of other classroom aids, would seem to be a matter of faculty member discretion regarding effective pedagogy.

There remains advocacy which is clearly unrelated to the course subject matter. We have heard of examples in which instructors lecture students about moral and political issues which have nothing to do with the course—a math teacher telling students the Iraq War is wrong, a geology professor telling students that abortion is immoral, or an English professor telling students that tax policies are unfair. There seems to be wisdom in the AAUP's policy and common university rule that professors should not introduce material unrelated to the subject matter.

Yet a strict prohibition on advocacy irrelevant to the course is also excessive. This would rule out icebreaking anecdotes and jokes. It would also prevent professors from giving general tips about study habits and college life that, though relevant to their students' lives, are not related to the course's subject. It is commonplace to expect that educators will do things such as serve as models for action and mentor students. If these things are not to be viewed as unfortunate deviations from the learning of subject matter, then it must be acknowledged that professors should have some leeway to depart from course content.

Rather than strictly ruling out material unrelated to course themes, a better guideline is Peter Markie's (1996) suggestion that "we may advocate a position only if our doing so does not prevent us from covering the course's assigned content" (p. 295). It would be wrong to spend significant amounts of time and energy in a math class discussing the morality of the Iraq War or abortion. It's not wrong because professors promise not to touch on anything but math, but because students are promised that the professor will teach them math. This principle would serve to rule out dedicating any significant amount of time to discussing political or moral issues not related to the class. Even if advocacy is relevant, such as making a case against the Vietnam War in an American history class, it can be excessive in its use of class time.

In addition to the need to cover what is promised, Markie (1996) argues that educators "may only advocate a position if we have good reason to believe that that position is correct" (p. 297). Educators should not use their authority to assert things beyond their expertise. This stricture would also rule out the introduction of much material irrelevant to the subject.

The AAUP code of ethics states that professors should specifically not introduce material that is "controversial" as well as unrelated to the subject. It's not clear why only controversy is excluded, but some justification might be found in the arguments raised by Markie. Controversy does tend to lead to long and heated debates and distract from covering course material. It is also less likely that professors can have good reasons to believe that they are right about controversial issues than about less controversial matters, such as valuable study habits.

Although the case against advocacy so far has not been decisive, there are some reasons to think that neutrality should be adopted as a basic intent of educators, at least regarding controversial moral, political, and religious issues that are not necessary to the educational process. First, although advocacy isn't necessarily indoctrination, it is particularly likely to slip into indoctrination. In defending his or her own views, a professor is likely to fail to note shortcomings or countenance contrary evidence and arguments. The view is likely to be presented as possessing a higher degree of certainty than it really has and be rendered prematurely immune to further testing in the minds of students. When an idea is presented as clearly a professor's own view or as the only reasonable alternative, students may be intimidated from pursuing other possibilities. Since advocacy tends to lead to indoctrination, this is a good reason to avoid it. Even if advocacy does not undermine students' ability to think for themselves, the professor taking sides may prematurely close down discussion or lead to strategic silence on the part of students who do not wish to hurt their grades or get into an argument with a professor.

A second reason to think advocacy is unwise is that it is likely to fail. If students have not learned good moral sense by college, it may be too late for professors to influence them. In his critique of the recent effort to teach values at the university level, Stanley Fish (2003) argues that the moral improvement of students is an educational aim for which professors are unprepared and possess a poor track record. Fish notes that the lessons students take from classes are frequently different than those intended by faculty. He cites a professorial experience of being thanked by a former student for having taught the student some principle that became a beacon in the student's life, when one in fact dedicated one's career to teaching just the opposite view. Fish's conclusion is that professors should "aim low"—at student's comprehension of facts and theories—instead of at the lofty target of their moral improvement.

Furthermore, it could be argued that if advocacy is done in a nonindoctrinating manner it has few advantages over neutrality. A neutral presentation of evidence and arguments on each side of an issue allows for critical thinking and rational debate, and should allow the truth to emerge in the course of discussion and reflection. Although Baumgarten's (1982) defense of the Socratic method fails to demonstrate that there is anything inherently immoral about advocacy, it could be argued that by being relatively certain to avoid controversy and indoctrination, a neutral approach to teaching remains a wise and sound course.

From Neutrality to Advocacy of Humanity

Although there are practical and principled reasons for neutrality in the classroom, other arguments justify considerable advocacy. First, there is reason to think that professors should promote certain basic, widely held values beyond those necessary for the educational process. For example, teachers can and should promote the values of human life, liberty, equality, and the alleviation of suffering. The development of such values is one aim of a liberal education. Philosophers of education have long held that developing good character in students is one of the central goals of education, alongside and complementary to those of cultivating knowledge of the world and of independent, critical reflection. Plato's (1980) dialogue, "Protagoras," contains an impassioned plea by the title character that virtue can and should be taught. At the end of the dialogue, Socrates is described as awed and utterly persuaded by this position. Although Socrates' dialectical method is treated as exemplary by advocates of a neutral classroom such as Baumgarten (1982), Socrates probably would have considered the proposal that professors strive for neutrality absurd. In the dialogues reported by Plato, Socrates himself is far from neutral. He engages in questioning to push conversation toward desired, better conclusions about truth and justice. He stops asking questions only when an adequate conclusion is reached. Similarly, one finds Socratic professors today steering dialogue with their questions and intervening more firmly when views they consider foolish begin to take hold of the discussion.

The idea that education should produce virtuous citizens has not withered under the critical analysis of enlightenment modernity. Locke

(1693/1997) and Jefferson (1781/1964) concurred that a comprehensive education includes moral instruction. While Rousseau's (1755/1979) classic description of Emile's education emphasizes that children should not be trained to fulfill social roles, it also depicts a central purpose of education as awakening and cultivating natural sentiments, especially sympathy for others. In the 20th century, the great debate in the philosophy of education was between John Dewey's (1938/1963) progressive, instrumentalist, and hands-on philosophy of education and Robert Hutchins's (1953) traditional liberal education. Despite different emphases regarding method, both agreed that education should attempt to produce citizens prepared to participate in a democratic, civil society.

Values advocacy in education is also supported by the mission of universities. Postsecondary education (particularly at public universities, but also at private colleges) is supported by public funding. It is reasonable for the public to expect that its educational expenses will be used to cultivate social virtues and a civil society. This does not involve brainwashing or indoctrinating students—which is presumably not itself desired by the public. Instead it requires attempting to model, cultivate, and persuade students of the value of virtues such as civility, tolerance, benevolence, and creativity that contribute to the social good. Although some students and parents might expect an education which is solely for the personal benefit of the student, a just society ought not allow educational resources to be devoted to the procurement and maintenance of privilege by those with access.

Of course, the nature of social justice is contested. The most influential modern accounts of justice have viewed social norms as justified insofar as they could be agreed to by citizens asked to select principles that all must live by (Rawls, 1971). One could only endorse self-interest insofar as one was willing to have all others do the same. In reflecting on such a contract, most would select basic values to be taught in schools.

Some values are nearly universally recognized by most people on reflection, regardless of their religious, cultural, and intellectual backgrounds. For example, civility, honesty, truthfulness, equality and nondiscrimination, integrity, fairness, nonharm, and mutual toleration are almost universally valued. Not only is there a wide-ranging consensus on such basic values, but they are also probably required for any kind of functioning society. It could be argued that such principles have a validity akin to those of mathematical axioms or scientific paradigms, and can be rightly taught as knowledge. Most classroom advocacy probably involves the recommendation of such basic values. For example, literary works and historical accounts are chosen to depict racism, sexism, poverty, and other social problems. Although the study of such works may also have other artistic, factual, and theoretical value, one reason for assigning them is that they can be used to teach values such as tolerance and understanding of difference, empathy for the suffering of others, and concern for social equality.

Nonetheless, some would object to teaching such basic values. One might object that if such values are truly universal then there is no need to teach them. Richard Rorty (1989) argues that the teaching of basic values is appropriate for K–12 education, but not higher education. Subjecting adult students to platitudes about equality, fairness, and integrity may waste their time or insult them and cause resistance to the educational process. Furthermore, a focus on the ways in which literature, history, and politics demonstrate moral principles may detract from the consideration of more complex questions about the interpretation of texts and social forces, which lack a straightforward moral message.

Although it is true that most students recognize the validity of basic values in the abstract, they lack awareness of their application. Professorial advocacy should not principally be aimed at convincing students of the abstract truth that racial discrimination is wrong, something about which most already agree. Rather, it should demonstrate the long and ongoing history of discrimination. Although students know in general that poverty is a bad thing, they are frequently not aware of what kinds of poverty exist here and abroad. Education ought to spark awareness of the extent to which the world is at odds with basic norms.

Another important task of values education is cultivating a better understanding of widely held values. Moral principles can be ambiguous and their concrete implications unclear. Discussions in courses about medical ethics, business ethics, environmental ethics, and the ethics of warfare largely consist of debates over the application of moral principles to particular issues. In teaching "applied ethics," professors have a twofold purpose. One is to foster students' ability to intelligently, critically, and independently analyze and debate about difficult ethical dilemmas. A key lesson in this goal is that the right answers are not obvious and there are good reasons in favor of more than one answer. Professorial neutrality as opposed to advocacy suits this goal well.

However, a second goal of ethics education is to foster student understanding of and sensitivity to the ethical considerations at stake in medicine, business, and war. Business students in ethics classes frequently display skepticism about whether corporations have any moral obligations to the community, such as to provide safe products, a clean environment, and good working conditions. Students in courses on war are frequently dubious about whether military decision-making can be judged morally—for example, whether there are any ethical limits on what a state can do in its own self-interest or whether it is wrong to kill civilians. Professors who seek to prepare students for humane, civil, professional action cannot be entirely neutral about such issues. Faculty would fail in their duty if they did not attempt to cultivate basic moral sensitivity in sometimes cynical college students. Faculty teaching in pre-professional programs in military academies and business programs have a particular responsibility to cultivate adherence to codes of conduct. Similar points hold for the teaching of future professionals in medicine, law, social service, and journalism—though students of such professions more readily accept that they have ethical obligations. Indeed insofar as any higher education is citizenship education, one of its goals is moral instruction. Professors would also fail in their duties if they did not serve as advocates for humanitarian values such as refraining from killing civilians, cheating clients, or breaching confidentiality. Professors should attempt to design lectures and nudge discussion in favor of humane responses to social issues by using examples, arguments, and a presentation style which make clear and compelling the implications for human well-being.

These dual missions in teaching about ethics, society, and politics create a dilemma for educators. The intellectual goals of ethics courses (even in preprofessional programs) demand that students be allowed, even encouraged, to question moral obligations. Higher education should not become mere training for right action. On the other hand, education should not be indifferent to virtue and principle. A good education will contain elements of both values-cultivation and open-ended critical ethical dialogue.

In addition to awareness and recognition of basic values and threats to them, education can also foster student ethical concern and motivation. Although information about social problems is available through the news, such facts do not necessarily create an affective response. Literature, anthropology, and legal and ethical case studies in the classroom can raise sensitivity to and concern about violations of humanitarian principles to which students might otherwise be hardened. Education ought to result in motivation to act on the basis of what is learned. Though certainly Fish (2003) is right that we cannot guarantee that students will act, education can and should encourage interest in improving the world. Political and ethical education ought to create an interest in social affairs and a disposition to act on the basis of moral and political understanding.

Professorial advocacy is not only acceptable but obligatory when students directly challenge basic norms such as nondiscrimination and tolerance. To use examples common in today's classrooms, if students make antigay or anti-Arab slurs and insults, professors have a responsibility to indicate the indefensibility of such statements. Intervention is needed, in part, to protect students in the denigrated group from psychological harm and exclusion. Although students can speak up for themselves, some do not speak against an aggressive antagonist or a hostile and skeptical majority. Students may not wish to expose their own background, particularly in the face of manifest intolerance. Even when students are prepared to defend themselves, heated personal disputes may spiral into increasing conflict. Although dealing with such tension can have pedagogical value, it can also risk physical harm and prolonged antagonism which distracts from the goals of the course.

Although educational disturbance is one reason to advocate for civic virtues (Simon, 1994), the learning of other material need not be in jeopardy to justify advocacy. If a professor could be assured that allowing racist and sexist remarks would not harm the educational process—perhaps because there are no denigrated students present or because the instructor knows the individuals present are sufficiently hardened to discrimination—it would still be wrong for professors to fail to advocate equality. The greatest educational reason to challenge such statements is not that they distract from student opportunities to learn objective facts, but rather that professors should promote moral as well as factual truth in the classroom.

There are various ways of confronting discrimination in the classroom and of advocating humanitarian values. The most effective are teaching methods which don't dogmatically shout down benighted students or present moralizing lectures. It is more effective to use questions to illustrate problems with offensive views asserted by students. Such questions can serve to indicate professorial disagreement and suggest that students be more careful and responsible about what they say. Such a Socratic approach does not avoid advocacy—it intends to move students toward some conclusions and away from others—but it does so in a way which engages, instead of silences, the rational response of the student.

Markie (1994), while not opposed to advocacy in the classroom, raises another objection to advocacy of basic values in the classroom. He notes that universities need not fulfill their duties to foster basic norms through classroom teaching. Rather than teach the values of toleration, nondiscrimination, and humane treatment in the classroom, colleges could arrange other workshops and student programs designed to instill values. This would save time in the classroom and help professors avoid indoctrination and off-putting moralizing. Such programs might be particularly effective to guarantee that all students gain experience with ethical issues that frequently arise on campuses, particularly regarding sexual relationships and encounters with diversity. However, these programs do not serve as a complete alternative to classroom engagement of moral issues. Such programs are frequently crammed into a short time in welcome week, likely to be quickly forgotten. Taking them up again in the classroom allows for reinforcement. More importantly, raising norms in the context of coursework brings them to life, demonstrating their relevance and complexities in their application.

Advocacy and Evaluation: Downgrading for Moral and Political Incorrectness?

If professors may legitimately advocate for particular values, principles, and virtuous character traits, this raises the question of whether professors should grade students for their morality. Markie (1994) suggests that if education in virtue is a course goal, then professors ought to grade students' moral achievement. One might argue that since we do not grade it, it should not be taught. To grade virtue seems highly problematic. To use the force of grades to compel students to exhibit particular values moves closer to indoctrination. Furthermore, insofar as the judgment of values is uncertain and requires difficult (if not entirely subjective) judgment, it is problematic for professors to give grades on this basis. A central worry about values advocacy is that it will entail discrimination against students who disagree with the professor. The Students' Bill of Rights (Tennessee Senate Bill 1117, 2005), seeking to protect students from faculty advocacy, asserts that students should have "the right to expect that they will be graded solely on the basis of their reasoned answers and appropriate knowledge of the subjects they study and that they shall not be discriminated against on the basis of their political or religious beliefs."

Two responses can be made to this "grading virtue" problem. First, it isn't necessary to have everything which is taught be graded. Some things which students can and should learn are not easily evaluated—thoughtfulness and civility in participation and interest in the subject matter. Grading such things is problematic, because it requires subjective and contextual judgment and interpretation of student motives and intentions. While it is not clear whether the exhibition of the virtues of inquiry should be graded, few would question whether educators should attempt to model and encourage such behaviors.

On the other hand, it is sometimes valid to grade students for their display of virtue. Many professors can and do judge and reward good classroom participation. "Good participation" is not only informed, relevant, and insightful, but also civil, thoughtful, and productive. Although assessment of the quality of participation requires far from scientifically objective judgments, such evaluations are not without basis. If intolerance and incivility are part of student's belief system, then professors can justifiably grade students down for their morality and politics—at least insofar as it is expressed in the class.

In further contradiction to the Students' Bill of Rights, it is also sometimes appropriate to grade students' moral, political, and religious assertions. Professors—especially in the field of ethics, but also in the other humanities and social sciences—have to evaluate student arguments on ethical and public policy issues. Any argument for a particular policy or individual course of action involves normative principles, either explicit or implicit. Arguments for greater antiterrorist measures involve the claim that preventing killing is good; arguments for universal health care involve the claim that inequality and suffering are bad. Arguments also involve factual claims, e.g., that particular measures would reduce terrorism or suffering. Many factors should be included in grading a student's paper—including clarity, coherence, and originality—but it is also appropriate to evaluate the plausibility of normative assumptions as well as factual ones.

Considering the plausibility of assumptions can be seen in an example. A common argument in students' ethics papers is that allowing people to die or be killed can be a good thing because it helps to control the earth's population. Thus, students sometimes say that AIDS, lack of health care, terrorism, war, and natural disasters are good because they reduce the human population. Sometimes it is stated that this is in turn desirable because it will ease environmental degradation and resource depletion. A philosophy which says that students should not be criticized for their moral or political views would imply that such a proposal cannot be criticized. However, it seems clear that it should be criticized as morally problematic and implausible. Most do not accept that it is good to allow some to die to increase the survival chances of others. One might criticize the argument as self-contradictory: It is good for people to die to prevent overcrowding, and prevention of overcrowding is good because it prevents death. The argument seems to rely on an implicit assumption that the lives of some people are worth more than the lives of others. Professors who downgrade students for relying on such arguments penalize students for the assertion of implausible values and do so rightly.

It could be argued that the students are and should be penalized only for their faulty reasoning, especially their failure to make their assumptions explicit. After all, a central component of instruction in critical thinking is to educate students to be explicit about their reasoning. If professors can simply grade the completeness of students' arguments, then they need not grade the validity of moral premises. Yet when educators criticize a student for not clarifying and defending an assumption, they do so because the assumption in question is implausible or controversial, as in assertions of the expendability of human life or of human inequality. Such premises require additional defense, including a response to obvious objections. Premises about widely recognized empirical facts or humanistic values do not require the same exposition and defense. Although professors should grade students primarily for the quality of their defense of their views, the nature of the views partially determine what form of defense is needed. Logical form and moral content are not entirely separable such that one can grade only the former.

Students must show awareness of their assumptions and offer additional defense or explanation when assumptions are implausible. If it is a student's moral, political, or religious position to hold implausible views without justification, the student cannot expect to merely assert this view in order to receive a good grade. Some professors have been shocked to hear the student question "Do you want a paper that is well reasoned or that expresses my actual view?" One hopes that such dilemmas can be minimized in education, but in argumentative essays it is clear that teachers should grade on the basis of critical inquiry rather than sincerity.

Our argument must acknowledge that a student who gives an intelligent, consistent, well-explained defense of values and views that the professor finds problematic or even repugnant deserves a good grade. Professors may at times face intelligent racists and sexists in their classes who are prepared to argue for their views, perhaps citing statistical support for discriminatory proposals. In writing such a paper, a student shows awareness of the controversiality of his or her assertions and attempts to respond to ethical objections. Because this student has satisfied the intellectual demands of the assignment, he or she must be given a good grade. Of course, if the professor disagrees with the conclusion, he or she must believe the paper to contain some error in its assumptions or reasoning (Wilder, 1978). Yet a paper can be well explained and argued even if it is ultimately mistaken. Liberal professors should be prepared to give As to a young George Will or William Bennett, and conservative professors have to give good marks to a John Kenneth Galbraith or Noam Chomsky.

When students uncritically assert implausible values, it is incumbent upon professors to not simply give a bad grade, but also to attempt to explain the problem to the student. As argued in the chapter on grading, while grades are meant to be an evaluation of the quality of student work, the professor's response to student work should contribute to student improvement, including their moral and political reflection.

Advocacy on Controversial Matters

The argument so far supports classroom advocacy which helps to promote concern for and awareness of threats to uncontroversial human values. It rejects the case for strict instructional neutrality. This leaves unresolved the question whether professors may advocate for their views about more controversial matters, such as whether the Iraq War was justified, abortion is morally acceptable, same sex marriage should be legalized, or God exists. It is professors' defense of and attempt to sway students on such issues which has lead to criticism of professorial advocacy. Conservative critics of liberal academics are less concerned with the promotion of general human values than with liberal professors' application of these values to support progressive conclusions about divisive social issues (Kupperman, 1996).

In such cases the costs, risks, and objections to advocacy are heightened. Such advocacy supports relatively questionable conclusions and is relatively likely to alienate students or create divisiveness in the classroom. Furthermore, because professors are advocating a position in which there is ideological competition, and in which they may be emotionally vested in their view's acceptance as correct, they are more likely to slip into indoctrination.

While such advocacy has costs and risks, we give it a conditional defense. First, for the educator to take a neutral stance on such issues would tend to give students the relativistic message that no answers are better or closer to the truth than any others regarding moral, political, and religious questions. This is to promote a dubious doctrine that students are too ready to embrace out of laziness, defensiveness, and post-modern cultural influences. A neutral instructor could try to preempt this relativistic implication by notifying students that her own refusal to advocate a position is due to the neutrality required by her role and not because of personal indifference or the lack of objectively correct answers. Yet such an explicated neutrality still has the disadvantage of failing to model a concerned but responsible defense of a position. Such modeling may contribute to the educational goal of creating engaged and independent citizens. A professor who never advocates conclusions can model critical reasoning but not commitment. The neutral professor might try to further close this "commitment gap" by giving examples of sincere engagement by other intellectuals and activists. For example Pope John Paul II's opposition to abortion could be contrasted with the arguments and stories of feminists defending abortion rights—thereby giving students models of engagement to choose from. However, such pedagogy still has a cost. Students would not encounter flesh and blood individuals taking a stand on contemporary issues—commitment would only exist on paper or in classroom videos, not in professors.

Students' education can be enhanced by an awareness of their professors' individual backgrounds and beliefs. Students desire to know where their professors are "coming from"; having a sense of the professor's individuality and humanity helps many relate to the subject matter. If students do not get a sense of their professor's interest in the subject matter, they may not be able to relate to it themselves. In her essay, "A Teacher Is Either a Witness or a Stranger," Penny Gold (1996) argues that effective teaching is in large part self-disclosure. To approach a topic sincerely and in depth, a professor must unveil and reveal her own thinking on it. Gold argues that the cost of substituting a neutral stance for one's own genuine view is too high. The instructor who lacks passion and conviction becomes insincere and shallow. Many of us recall that our most influential professors were advocates, passionately and idiosyncratically defending particular approaches to intellectual and social issues. Indeed, one suspects that critics of advocacy forget their own academic influences and, to the extent that they are engaged professors, probably fail to heed their own ethical admonishments.

There is a risk that such personalization and advocacy will result in the curriculum being too much about the professor and not enough about the subject matter. We are familiar with professors with distinctive personalities cultivating a following of "disciples." We may wonder whether students in such a professor's classes would not be better off with an instructor committed to leaving conclusions open. Yet there are safeguards that can and should be taken against this, short of rejecting advocacy. First, when advocating, professors must remember the norms against indoctrination. If professors attempt to foreclose questions and challenges to the views they defend, then they probably do as much or more disservice to adoring followers than to those who are inclined to disagree with them. Second, students should be encouraged to take a wide range of courses with different professors—both in satisfying their general education requirements and within their majors—so that they encounter professors advocating a range of different positions. Philosophy students benefit from encountering professors who defend libertarianism, existentialism, Marxism, and feminism. They probably learn more by encountering advocates of diverse positions than they do with taking classes from a series of professors who all present "neutral" accounts of the field.

Of course, there is also room for professors who refrain from advocacy on most or all controversial issues. Individual instructors may pursue neutrality for various reasons. Some may be genuinely uncertain about the proper conclusions on controversial social issues and thus feel that there is no clear correct view to promote. Others may be personally predisposed to a nondirective model of teaching, or be convinced of the pedagogical advantages of teachers refraining from articulating a definitive viewpoint. Most professors probably withhold their own views for most of the classroom discussion about most issues. They allow student discussion to be the last word on some issues, while stating their own conclusions about other matters. There are various ways of advocating or indicating what one takes to be the right view. Rather than lecturing on the superiority of a position, one can present it at the end of a discussion as a possible solution. Instructors must balance the pedagogical advantages and disadvantages of the different forms of advocacy and neutrality.

As Felicia Ackerman (1996) argues, students are better served by various faculty teaching in the manners that best suits them, rather than having all of them embrace identical Socratic pedagogy. If teachers avoid indoctrination within a classroom and if the curriculum involves an encounter with educators who adopt a range of views and educational strategies, then students are not done a disservice.

Classroom advocacy is valuable not only in engaging students, but also in promoting underrepresented views. The academy has traditionally served as a forum in which new ideas are developed and undervalued perspectives and theories are promoted. One of the main arguments for academic freedom is that it facilitates the development and discovery of new ideas. Although professorial *research* is probably the most common locus for the development of new theories, discussions in the classroom help to test and revise new ideas. The classroom is a principal venue through which such ideas can be introduced into the public sphere, leading to social change. Although the academy certainly has not been the only source of movements such as feminism, antiracism, peace, environmental, and human and workers' rights, it has been a major one.

Advocating unproven, controversial views is defensible to the extent that professors have reasons to believe that the positions they advocate are not taken as seriously as the evidence and arguments for them warrants. This kind of advocacy promotes new or minority ideas to provide a kind of balance for the students' normal intellectual climate. This advocacy need not take the form of indoctrination; indeed it can emphasize particular arguments and evidence, without attempting to thwart dissent. Professors commonly engage in devil's advocacy in order to push students to defend their everyday views. Professorial defense of unpopular ideologies can encourage students to take these views more seriously. In this context, advocacy fosters rather than inhibits student intellectual inquiry. One might object that a principle which states that we may advocate for our ideas which are undervalued essentially gives license to advocate for any and all of our beliefs. After all, don't we all think that society would do better to take all of our ideas more seriously? On the contrary, professors are sometimes able to recognize that the ideas and values we are concerned with are given sufficient credence in society or the academic community such that one has no reason to offer it additional favor or weight in the classroom. In liberal arts colleges and humanities programs in which liberal and progressive values are emphasized, there is little reason for professors to attempt to promote such values. However, for professors who teach in conservative schools and business schools, the case is different. Professors have an obligation to not waste time "preaching to the choir." Education should broaden student perspectives and stimulate their reflection. This requires the questioning of dogmatically held views and the presentation of possible alternatives. Paradoxically, when professors do come under criticism for their advocacy, this is a sign that education is serving an important function in challenging received views. The advocacy which fails students as autonomous individuals is that which perpetuates uncritical adherence to views which they are predisposed to by national culture or subcultures in which students move.

Judgments about when advocacy is justified are complicated by the fact that there are different levels at which ideas or values can be underrepresented. A view can be undervalued in the class, in the wider community, or society as a whole. Some colleges and courses will be filled with students with countercultural values. Socialist, feminist, antiwar, and other views that are poorly represented in society may be disproportionately present in the classroom. In such cases, contributing to student critical reflection indicates that the socialist, feminist, antiwar professor should play "devil's advocate." Advocacy could only be defended as needed to further advance the new ideas being developed by students, which are needed in the community outside of school. Ideally, professors will find some balance between promoting activism and promoting reflective thinking. There will inevitably be room for judgment about when a view is underrepresented in the education of a group of students and warrants advocacy. This means that on some controversial issues, professors will be justified in advocating on either side of the issue. For example, professors may emphasize arguments for or against the Iraq War, abortion, or the existence of God. These are the kinds of conclusions in which professorial advocacy must take pains to avoid indoctrination, acknowledge uncertainty, and encourage student discussion and debate. The most common and justifiable form of advocacy is negative advocacy, which attempts to explain why commonly accepted arguments fail to prove a particular conclusion. Yet making a positive case that a particular argument justifies a conclusion is itself sometimes justified. In order to determine when to advocate for what views and how, professors will have to take into account the effects in the classroom as well as the social contexts for the issues under discussion, leading to difficult judgments. Neither a blanket prohibition nor endorsement of advocacy is appropriate.

Conclusion

Our discussion of advocacy yields the following proposal:

1) Professors should avoid indoctrination in their advocacy. In particular professors should not:
   - Attempt to influence students to believe things without regard for the evidence
   - Coerce student agreement or silence to secure the prevalence of their own views
   - Lie about or distort material

2) Professors must support independent intellectual inquiry. In particular they should:
   - Make clear that different views and questions are welcome
   - Present a balanced discussion of reasonable alternatives and relevant considerations regarding issues discussed

3) Professors should avoid advocacy which prevents the accomplishment of course goals.

4) Professors should only advocate positions which they have good reason to believe are correct.

5) Professors should only advocate when they have reason to believe advocacy will contribute to student development. The value of advocacy may include:
   - Fostering values necessary for education and inquiry

- Teaching basic humanitarian principles and virtues necessary for good citizenship
- Promoting views that are not taken sufficiently seriously by students

6) The pedagogical value of advocacy in item 5 should outweigh any costs of advocacy in class time or the unintentional alienation or intimidation of students.

3

Conflicts of Interest

Classically a conflict of interest involves the use of one's proper authority in one area of responsibility to unduly influence, or appear to, another area of one's responsibility. For example, a mayor who is responsible for vetting contracts for city projects is involved in a conflict of interest when a company to which he or she is officially engaged vies for and is awarded a city contract. In this example, it appears that the mayor has used his or her proper authority as mayor for personal benefit. The mayor's role as a company official is at odds with the requirements of the mayoral office to review contacts based on their merits. Personal commitments and interests can undermine a professional's judgment of and motivation to pursue the public good. Even if a professional continues to engage in good faith service to the community and his or her clients, the mere appearance of a conflict of interest can undermine the legitimacy of decision-making.

In terms of conflicts of interests in the academy, the classical notion can be operative. A professor would be at pains to explain, for example, how fairness in grading was maintained when his or her child or relative was enrolled in his or her class. Responsibilities as a parent or relative are confounded with responsibilities as a professor in the classroom context. The same applies when a professor is involved romantically with a student who is enrolled in his or her class (see Chapter 6 for treatment of this issue). In these cases, firewalls can be established to support fairness—using objective tests, consulting with other professors when grading the student's responses to subjective tests, ensuring the confidentiality of testing materials prior to their use—but the appearance of favoritism may be difficult to overcome, and the appearance of favoritism is not a slight consideration when professors consider the general perception of their character.

Without diminishing the importance of the classical notion of conflicts of interest, we think professors struggle with much more complex and nuanced conflicts of interest in teaching. In fact, a variety of faculty interests and commitments can prevent faculty from consistently and conscientiously carrying out their obligations as teachers. Professors' teaching duties can conflict with their general interests as human beings and specific commitments as academics. Professors have personal interests and needs for which they may use time that could be otherwise spent honing a lecture or consulting teaching resources.

In the most egregious cases, laziness, irresponsibility, or disengagement—combined with a lack of oversight of faculty—can result in professors intentionally doing the minimum amount of work possible. We are familiar with stories of professors who merely show up to teach their classes (perhaps even regularly missing them or arriving late) without spending any significant time preparing for class, giving feedback, or making themselves available to assist students. The common anecdote of professors pulling out yellowed notes suggests that sometimes teaching commitment is lacking or eroded. In such cases, there is little question that professors have placed personal interest above teaching obligations.

It is difficult to specify, of course, how much time and energy a college professor should put into teaching. While showing up for class and office hours are minimal and objectively measurable standards, it is impossible to establish (much less enforce) definitive standards for how much time should be spent preparing lessons, improving pedagogy, grading papers, and advising students. It is clear, however, that a professor can commit too little to such activities and consequently fail to teach well and shortchange his or her students. Professors must teach at least adequately to meet the legitimate expectations of students and the requirements of their profession. However, there is a prima facie duty to teach as well as one can, and to continue to improve one's lessons and methods even after they are adequate. In general professors should use their time and energy to further education. How time is allocated will always be non-ideal, leaving the professor to realize that either his or her research or teaching (or likely both) could have been better had he or she allocated more time to it. In making these judgments, faculty are responsible to avoid allowing personal incentives to lead them to overemphasize research at the expense of teaching.

Some attention to self-interest is, of course, legitimate and indeed necessary. Professors can legitimately expect to take time to eat, sleep, and recreate. Denial of basic needs would not only be too much to ask of educators, but by undermining the educator's physical and mental health would probably ultimately undermine the quality of instruction itself. At times professors may face unusual personal burdens, such as illness or a role in caring for an aging or disabled family member. In such cases, the satisfaction of personal interests and needs may make it particularly difficult to adequately satisfy, much less excel in, teaching. Of course, professors may request leaves of absence. Unfortunately the nature of teaching is such that it is difficult for a professor to find a substitute who knows the material and is familiar with the course structure. Thus while asking for leave acknowledges the problem of inadequate time and attempts to correct that problem, possibly sacrificing some of the professor's income, the professor's absence may still leave students poorly served. This is not to say that professors must always choose their students over themselves and their family. It is to say that sometimes instructors must make difficult choices between their responsibilities. The obligation to teach remains even in the face of other personal obligations. Professors generally can be expected to put up with some hardship to show up for class, plan lessons, and continue to teach well during difficult periods.

Regarding Research

A different form of self-interest is more peculiar to and endemic in the academic profession. Those with an academic calling have intellectual interests and personal commitment to a field of study, the exploration of which becomes an open-ended, lifelong project. Research demands professorial energy and attention but it also provides personal fulfillment. The pursuit of knowledge and the feeling of having made progress toward the truth are pleasurable and satisfying. Because research engages their discipline at the highest and most challenging level, as intellectuals faculty are likely to find it more satisfying than teaching. Furthermore, research is more likely to lead to external goods such as honors, awards, grants, promotions, and rais-es. Time spent doing research is more likely to contribute to career advancement and financial remuneration than time engaged in improving pedagogy. Given these interests and incentives, faculty frequently try to maximize time spent working on their own projects. This means minimiz-ing time spent teaching—including cutting back on the amount of reading and writing assigned, the detail of lesson plans, and comments on students' work. Faculty may even come to resent time spent teaching and resent their students for the time demands they make.

The choice of research over teaching is not a classic conflict of inter-est. Research, unlike a romantic relationship with a student or the exploitation of student labor, is a duty of academics alongside that of teaching and "service"—these three are thought to comprise the funda-mental duties of faculty. It is well known that not only at classic research institutions but even at institutions traditionally designated "teaching colleges," publication is required for tenure and promotion. Professors are not simply tempted to spend time doing research that could be used for teaching, they are obliged to do so.

How common is this strand of self-interest, which allows one duty to overshadow, even eclipse, other duties? Bergquist (1992) says, "Many fac-ulty and administrators enter American colleges and universities precise-ly because they wish to be left alone to pursue their own teaching, research, writing, or ideas" (p. 170). The desire to "be left alone" suggests a self-interest in which one does not wish to be interrupted by other duties. The attachment to one academic duty to the virtual exclusion or grudging acknowledgment of others suggests that self-interest is the car-dinal element that motivates professors. "By common report," Bennett (1998) notes, "many faculty are already disposed toward self more than others—toward aggressive pursuit of individual interests rather than a common good" (p. 2).

We suspect that disproportionate interest in research as opposed to teaching is nurtured in graduate school. The focus of graduate school is scholarship, so graduate schools prepare students to become scholars, without much regard for teaching and service. Until they become profes-sors, graduate students are neither fully informed about the range of pro-fessorial responsibilities, nor given tools to perform them well. Of course, upon placement in faculty positions, new academics should become rapidly aware of the realities of their teaching obligations. The prospect of standing in front of roomfuls of students waiting for instruction has a way of inspiring teaching preparation. However, to the extent that research is still thought to play a disproportionate role in faculty advancement, self-interested concerns are likely to continue to motivate professors to cut corners in teaching.

If faculty have a responsibility to maintain their commitment to teaching in the face of their research interests and pressures, institutions have a responsibility to recognize, reward, and encourage good teaching relative to research. Benton (2005) agrees and asks penetrating questions about what he perceives as misdirected adulation of individuals in the academy:

> What would it be like if the humanities moved away from this culture of individual "genius" . . . . What if, instead, academe strove to embrace a culture of collaboration, organized around projects that do not showcase, first and foremost, the supposed brilliance of certain intellectual celebrities?
>
> What if . . . we began to support an ethic of service to our students and the profession instead of privileging and rewarding what, in the end, adds up to an epidemic of indifferent institutional citizenship masquerading as "excellence." (p. C4)

The tendency to overemphasize individual scholarship as opposed to contribution to education and institutional and professional citizenship warrants a rethinking of priorities by both professors and institutions.

We submit that most of the conflicts affecting classroom teaching stem from conflicts among legitimate obligations as to how to satisfy the package of responsibilities. At what point, for example, does a professor's engagement in research become an impediment in fulfilling other professorial duties, particularly if that research really is substantially informing the content the professor teaches? Because a person could legitimately use all his or her time to prepare for and improve teaching, how does a professor determine how to allocate scarce resources among competing professional obligations to maintain ethical integrity? In approaching the topic of competing professional obligations, we begin with a scenario that demonstrates ethical concerns related to competing professional obligations. Then we analyze the scenario to discuss conflicts of interest.

Scenario: Competing Professional Obligations

For the last few months, Professor Zil has anticipated the arrival of the book she now holds in her hands, her first published textbook. The publisher told her that this textbook has the potential to be a big seller, and already several universities have adopted the text for the upper-division course in Zil's specialty. Zil is proud of the book and takes it as a badge of honor that she developed the text with student input from her classes. After she drafted a chapter, she assigned it as required reading and asked students to mark the draft with any comments or questions they had. Zil compiled students' comments and used them to revise each chapter for publication. Writing the book was no easy task given her teaching load, so Zil on occasion had to cancel class to meet a publishing deadline—but she always gave her students work that would cover the topic for the missed classes. Once she also cancelled class to attend a conference at which she presented a paper related to the creative process of writing a textbook. She made arrangements with a colleague to be a guest lecturer while she was at the conference, but at the last minute, her colleague got sick. Zil considered substituting what would have been a hastily prepared library assignment but decided in the end to simply cancel class. As book writing placed increasing demands on her time, she either skipped or arrived unprepared for committee meetings. She never realized how time consuming the writing would be, and she had to cut corners at home to meet publishing deadlines. She had planned to devote the previous summer to finishing the manuscript, but unexpected expenses created the need to teach during one of the five-week summer terms. She reduced the amount of work she normally expected of students for that summer session because she *had* to work on the book during every available moment. She wasn't even able to take a vacation! Starting the fall semester after the grueling summer schedule was a task—because she was exhausted she didn't feel at the top of her game that fall semester. Completing the page proofs within six weeks while teaching a full load put even more pressure on her, and certainly didn't allow for enough sleep. But she made it through the fall—even though she had to give some students incompletes because they turned in their projects at the last minute, after which she got sick and was unable to get her grading finished on time. She was able to get some rest over the holidays, catch up on most of her work, and begin planning for the spring semester. Now at the semester's start, she holds her labor of love in her hands, anticipating how she will use it when she teaches her upper-division specialty next fall.

Analysis of the Scenerio

This scenario is presented because we want to look at the complexities of a conflict of interest. It would be easy to simply investigate the potential conflict of interest that could occur when professors require their text in a class that they teach, but such a question needs to be placed in context. In fact, we see three issues in this scenario that require comment. First, should professors assign their texts to students in their classes? Second, to what extent should any professor use the resources of the classroom to produce a text? Third, to what extent should one aspect of a professor's responsibilities override other aspects?

Assigning One's Text

To begin answering the question about whether professors should assign their own texts to students in their classes, we can turn to Cahn (1986):

> I have heard it said that professors should not adopt texts they themselves authored or edited, since they would earn royalties on these required purchases. I see no conflict of interest in this practice, as long as the books chosen are, in fact, the most appropriate for the course. Shouldn't Ralph Ellison, when teaching a course in contemporary litera-ture, have the right to ask his students to read *Invisible*

Man? Whichever books are chosen, someone will earn royalties. The only genuine issue is whether the texts selected are pedagogically justifiable. (p. 16)

Cahn rightly assumes that the governing rule in making a determination about whether a professor should use his or her own text in a class the professor teaches is "whether the texts selected are pedagogically justifiable," but Cahn may be too quick to disentangle economic gain from pedagogical justification. That the two should be clearly separated is without question so that a potential conflict of interest regarding money is avoided. That Professor Zil or any professor can make that judgment objectively is another question and a difficult one to ascertain. Frankly, someone who has dedicated himself or herself to producing a book has a vested interest in the product of his or her labors, and to assume that one could easily disentangle one's pedagogical rationale from one's own interest would be naïve. If each text purchased yields the author several dollars, professors with moderate salaries have clear incentives to assign their books whenever plausible. Many authors may also enjoy having their own work be the center of classroom attention. Furthermore, the use of the book allows the professor to get feedback which may improve further editions. Even a professor seeking to act in good faith and follow Cahn's advice to assign the best text may have his or her own judgment subtly affected by personal interest. Part of the reason for avoiding conflicts of interest is that good intentions are not always sufficient for avoiding lapses in ethical judgment.

It could be argued that if a professor has produced a text, the professor would logically believe that this is the best text on the subject. If the professor thought it was flawed, she would have written it differently. However, this isn't always the case. Authors can fail to write well and adequately achieve all of their goals in producing a text. An author might recognize her own book as less well written or less suited to students' needs than a traditional text or a new alternative in the field. This is particularly likely if the professor teaches a course for which her own text is only tangentially related. The value that she believes her own work to have should be weighed against the greater relevance of other works.

For the assigning of one's own text to be justified, the professor's judgment of the relative quality and relevance of her own work must be reliable. She cannot necessarily assume that the fact that it was published means that it is good enough, much less the best work available. It would be a mistake to say that professors can never be trusted to make such judgments. Yet they must take pains to make an honest evaluation of their own work and its relevance. This might include getting a sense from reviewers and colleagues about the quality of the book as a course text, so as to gain some outside perspective.

If the problem of professorial bias can be addressed, there remains another important objection to the conflict of interest in assigning one's own text. Regardless of whether a professor assigns it because she reasonably judges it to be the best text available, it may appear to others that she is moved more by self-importance and the desire for remuneration. This potential conflict of perceptions about remuneration is particularly sensitive in public institutions during times of economic distress and distrustfulness regarding the professorial performance of state employees. Although conduct should be evaluated principally by the ethical nature of the act itself, if the perceptions of an act would have negative consequences, this can be a good reason to avoid the initial act (even if innocent or good).

In addition to the perceptions of those who fund higher education, students' perceptions of the moral integrity of the professor are at stake. Unlike government officials, students in a professor's class are certain to notice that the instructor has assigned her own text. If they believe the professor is trying to make money off them, this could be directly detrimental to the educational process. Skepticism about the professor could lead to cynicism regarding coursework and a loss of authority in the classroom.

Although there are real risks in a professor assigning her or his own book, we argue that these problems are surmountable and the risks tolerable. Professors can and should explain why they have assigned their own text—acknowledging that they may have some personal gain, while reassuring students that this is not their central motivation. Indeed many students probably would be surprised and disappointed to find that their professor had written a book on the course topic but not assigned it. Students would be deprived of an opportunity to have a dialogue directly with an author about his or her own work, and might suspect that the professor has held back what he or she thinks to be the best statement on the topic. In fact, it may be the case that professors tend to err on the side of holding their own work back too much, from worry over appearing arrogant and self-centered as much as from worry over the (generally slight) financial benefits (and perhaps excessive worry over the appearance of wrongdoing).

Professors can ethically require students to purchase texts the professors have published, but professors should inform students and make every effort to assure students that the reasons for using the text are pedagogically justified. This means, of course, that the mere assertion of pedagogical justification cannot be assumed to convince students that the text is pedagogically justified. Thus the quality of the text should prove to students that the professor's assertion of pedagogical justification rings true.

Some institutions of higher education have policies that allow a professor to assign his or her book, but the royalties for such sales must be donated to a charity or professional organization. Such policies serve to disentangle economic profit from pedagogical justification. At institutions with this policy, professors should announce it to the class; even when policy does not require such donations, professors might willingly ensure that they do not collect royalties on the copies sold to their students. It also might be pedagogically enlightening to explain to students just how little a professor earns per copy so that students become more aware of the economics of publishing.

Using Classroom Resources

The second issue—to what extent should a professor use the resources of the classroom to produce a text—begins with the assumption that the professor cannot help but make use of classroom resources when engaging in research. That is, both ideally and actually, the classroom is a place of insight. It is a commonplace observation that professors learn as much or more than their students in teaching courses. Professors learn from being pushed to articulate their own ideas, and from student questions, examples, and observations the professor learns additional perspectives, limits to his or her approach, and new paths of intellectual exploration.

To suggest that a professor should not in any way use the classroom to advance his or her own research would be to question a holistic view of professorial activities and radically minimize the influence of teaching and learning in the classroom on scholarly productivity, creating a false dichotomy between teaching and learning. This is nowhere more clear than when the professor writes a textbook. We would expect and hope that textbook authors would draw on their own experience teaching the topic and course in question, taking into account observations of student learning styles, interests, and problems, and noting more and less effective methods of presenting material. Students will inevitably be test cases for the treatment of issues and ideas in a text produced by their professor. Therefore the question is not whether professors may use classroom resources, but what the ethical limits are.

In Zil's case, two issues regarding the use of classroom resources can be explored. First, Zil required students to read and respond to drafts of her manuscript. Is such a practice justifiable? A first principle of teaching is that courses should be designed and assignments given to best promote learning. Zil must ensure that assigning students to read her chapters satisfies this requirement. However, promoting learning is not sufficient, because some activities better promote learning than others. For instance, it seems very unlikely that pouring over Zil's incomplete work is the best use of students' time—unless, of course, Zil is teaching a course on editing (a rare instance generally not applicable to most courses). Shouldn't Zil have students work on their own incomplete projects or give them a choice of texts to critically analyze so that they could pursue their own interests?

Indeed, Zil's decision to assign chapters of her own book for extensive feedback is so likely to be immediately useful to her that it is hard to think that this is not the main reason for this assignment. By assigning her own text, Zil seems to fail the "intended to and reasonably likely to maximize learning" test, and is most susceptible to the "rationalization" and "harmful appearances" objections. To put it in financial terms, assigning one's own book to a seminar of 10 students might get the professor 40 or 50 dollars in royalties (depending on the price of the text and the percent of royalties the author earns), but having students work as a team of editors for weeks might amount to thousands of dollars of free secretarial work. Therefore, using students to fulfill functions that are legitimately part of the professor's publishing responsibilities is questionable ethically and should generally be avoided.

However, it might be objected that if professors are justified sometimes in assigning their own texts, as we mentioned above, professors might legitimately ask for feedback on their work. If Zil rightly assigns critical analysis of other course texts, why not assign his or her own work? Requesting a critical response to her own work may be pedagogically justifiable. However, the professor must take care that the point of the assignment is to engage the student intellectually and not provide editorial feedback for the professor. Of course, editorial value may be a fortunate byproduct of critical analysis, which it would be wasteful for professors not to draw on, but the former purpose of engaging the student must guide assignment construction.

The assignment of commentary on one's own work will be more ethical the more choice students have in the matter, but much of the problem is that an assignment is by nature something that is not optional. However, professors can give choices of assignment topics, making it clear that they do not expect students to comment on their own material and that the professor does not expect help, much less praise, from the students. Professors could also invite voluntary feedback beyond course assignments, making it clear that this is not expected and that no extra credit will be given. Of course, the professor might not get much feedback, given student time constraints and preferences. However, some students might wish to contribute comments to help their instructor and future generations of students. If students do end up making helpful comments, either as part of an assignment or as volunteers, the professor should acknowledge their contributions in the text.

The thrust of these stipulations is that the professor-student relationship is protected so that the students are not seen as objects to be used for the professor's self-interest. That is, the primary purpose of the classroom enterprise is to promote learning, and when a scholarly project can promote that learning effectively, the use of classroom resources does not violate ethical conduct. If professors desire or need more assistance with their own work than occurs as a natural byproduct of students engaging material for their own purposes, the professor ought to hire students or others to work outside the confines of coursework.

The second issue regarding classroom resources is Zil's canceling classes and giving substitute assignments, and her adjustment of academic standards for her summer class. According to the scenario, these actions were taken because Zil's attention was directed toward completing her manuscript. Prima facie such actions constitute a conflict of interest because Zil is robbing Petrina to pay Paulina. She is literally shifting resources—namely her own energies—to complete a project that is robbing students of what Zil would customarily consider her rightful duties. Because Zil's primary responsibility in the class is to promote student learning, canceling class requires an important countervailing justification—the equivalent of an emergency. Giving assignments as substitutes for class meetings hardly qualifies as an adequate substitute for professorial presence. Indeed, changing class requirements during the summer due to publishing exigencies does not meet the test of pedagogical justification because the reason for changing the requirements was not that students would learn more.

Skipping class in order to work on research is unjustifiable. Research time is sufficiently flexible that faculty members should be able to work it around their teaching duties. Skipping class directly deprives students of education and fails to meet legitimate expectations and contractual obligations.

Yet it would probably be too much to ask that professors never cancel class for any research work. Attending a conference is a different matter. Presenting one's work and keeping abreast of developments in one's field is a necessary part of academic life. If Zil's conference is singularly relevant to her work, she may be justified in missing a day or two of class. Unlike research itself, conference meeting times are not flexible; professors may have to miss teaching to achieve research goals. However, to say that teaching can sometimes be missed for a presentation is not to give license to instructors to miss class whenever a conference would be of any value to their work. Regular absence from class for research reasons suggests that professors are traveling more than absolutely necessary and doing so to the detriment of student education.

Zil chose to teach an extra summer course at the same time she was engaged in a demanding research project. In essence, she overextended herself, and by so doing created an untenable situation that resulted in ethical misconduct. She failed to provide professional services she rightly should have because she made other commitments that conflicted with her classroom duties. Her primary responsibility, particularly during the compressed learning period of a five-week summer session, was to fulfill her duties to her students. By skipping classes to write, and possibly by choosing to attend an additional conference, her research commitments led her to fail in her duties to her students.

Overriding Other Duties

The third issue—to what extent one aspect of a professor's responsibilities overrides other aspects—is a knotty question that probably has to be determined on a case-by-case basis, partly because the mix of responsibilities varies for each professor, depending on the mission of an institution, a professor's success in acquiring particular resources (such as reassigned time), short- and long-term administrative assignments, health issues, and other variables. In Zil's case, however, the allocation of time and resources to producing the book should give us pause. Clearly she cut corners and shortchanged her students and her colleagues. Perhaps Zil could argue, on utilitarian grounds, that her shortchanging students today in order to finish her book will be more than made up for by the quality of the book. If it improves the education of future sections of her courses, then her cutting corners to finish the book may turn out to have been for the greater good. On the other hand, if Zil failed to finish the text, not only may it never be published, but she might be denied tenure and would not be able to serve students at all in the future. However, it is notoriously difficult to predict or evaluate such long-term consequences. Her book may not be useful to students or herself, or her tenure denial might result in the hiring of a better new professor as well as new opportunities for Zil. While long-term costs and benefits are uncertain, the failure to attend class as promised and serve students today is definitely a violation of duties.

Zil is violating her responsibilities not only as a professor but also as a committee member. Zil's failure to carry her weight on her committee assignments probably led others to do more than their share of the work or forced the committee to neglect some of its duties. If the committee did neglect some of its duties, others might have been injured because a policy was not enacted in a timely manner or a decision was not made that could have benefited students. Although a faculty member missing a few committee meetings will not always have an immediately detrimental impact, good-faith faculty participation in such activities is necessary for the maintenance and continual improvement of the university. Zil has a duty to be a good colleague, rightly considered an integral part of a faculty member's responsibilities (Connell & Savage, 1991).

Conclusions

Our scenario does not specify whether Zil negotiated changes in her obligations, which would certainly change our response to her conduct. If, for instance, she had gone to the chair of her department and explained her situation, she could have been granted release from her committee responsibilities and others might have taken up the work for which Zil was responsible. However, to unilaterally decide that work she was assigned can be set aside for her research appears to be an example of the failure of faculty service that concerns Bennett (2003).

We have constructed one scenario as an exemplar of how a professor might work through various issues related to potential conflicts of interest. We could have selected other details—using graduate students to conduct research in a laboratory, refusing to accept certain committee assignments, failing to post or be available during office hours because of other obligations, accepting employment outside of the university for various reasons, canceling classes or other obligations because of sick children or other family members, and so on. We hope that the scenario we have provided gives sufficient detail to discuss how the ethical principles we have used can be applied to particular circumstances in the professorial endeavor when conflicts of interest are in view. Clearly, however, conflicts of interest can be subtle; avoiding or minimizing conflicts of interest requires professional judgment, which involves careful thought and judicious consideration.

The Challenge of Professional Judgment

Underlying much of what we have said about legitimate conflicts among competing professional interests is the question of what place professional judgment plays in making decisions about how to appropriately balance professorial responsibilities. We admit that we have no easy answer to our own query. In fact, we don't think *any* easy answer is available for a variety of reasons.

First, as one wag noted, good judgment is born of bad judgment. Although bad judgment does not need to be the basis of good judgment in all cases, the truth remains that we can learn from our mistakes. Certainly we can learn from others' mistakes, and we can take good advice by soliciting it or accepting it when unsolicited, but bad personal experience can be a profoundly effective tutor. And *experience* is the operative term. In terms of teaching, part of what professors learn comes from the accretion of experience in the daily toil of teaching. It is one thing to advise beginning educators that students will ask a variety of questions, both brilliant and inane. It is yet another thing to recognize into which category a student's question fits and to know how to respond effectively. Conflicts among legitimate competing interests, such as how much time to devote to answering a student's question when the next lesson needs to be prepared, are matters of professional judgment honed over time. Beginning instructors may find a student's question so intriguing that they may neglect to prepare adequately for the next lesson, which would slight students in the class.

It appears that Zil, due to her lack of experience, did not comprehend the challenges that attend the production of a manuscript. In one sense, her lack of experience could be suspect. Doctoral programs require a dissertation, and doctoral students (and even many master's students) have produced a book-length manuscript, so the appeal to inexperience may be exaggerated. Nevertheless, producing a book-length manuscript for publication may not be as leisurely a process as writing a dissertation, so writing for publication can add a new dimension to professional judgment that often is learned through raw experience. Because this is Zil's first attempt at publishing a book, we might chalk up some of her ethical dilemmas to inexperience and hope that Zil adds to her storehouse of wisdom to make good decisions in the future. However, one could also ask whether Zil performed due diligence in undertaking a publishing project in relation to her other obligations. Did she ask others about their publishing experiences? Did she make realistic promises to the publisher? Did she attempt to renegotiate a publication date once she found that she was being overwhelmed? In short, what steps did she take before and during the publishing venture to ensure that she could meet all her professional obligations? Taking such steps and accepting the realities she learns about to plan her publishing venture prudently would mitigate the culpability of ethical lapses. "We need others," Bennett (2003) affirms, "because we can never know enough. What we do know is always partial and reflects limited perspectives and values. We also need others to keep us honest, to help us correct personal distortions and rationalizations" (p. 43).

Second, professional judgment (no matter how well honed) cannot deal adequately with some unexpected events. The best-laid plans of mice and prudent professors can and will be thwarted. Professional judgment is not perfect judgment. Although professionals can learn to avoid improvidence, they cannot guarantee future events. For instance, Zil did seek to have a professor represent her in class when she was going to be absent. That the substitute professor became incapacitated at the last minute does not count against Zil. We even commend her for making the decision not to construct hastily a library assignment that could have resulted in mere busywork. She may have had other options, such as asking the chair of her department for help or seeking advice from another colleague, but the time element in this situation mitigates against Zil's opportunity to weigh other options seriously. Did Zil's students suffer pedagogically because of this series of events? Certainly. They were deprived of the opportunity to learn from Zil. Was the cause of that deprivation Zil's ethical lapse? No—unless a chain of events, starting with Zil's acceptance of a publishing contract, are so interrelated that certain links in that chain cannot be considered as a unit. We take the position that even though Zil did act in many ways that were unethical regarding her teaching responsibilities, she did attempt to remedy a conflict between a legitimate duty to present her scholarship at a conference and a legitimate duty to provide instruction for her students. That her remedy failed was due to events beyond her control.

Third, professional judgment is context sensitive. The professional package of obligations is weighted in particular ways given the mission of the institution at which a professor is employed, the place a professor is in his or her career, and the latitude a professor has to make decisions about how to allocate his or her resources. For example, a professor at a research university should spend more time conducting research than a professor at an institute of higher education in which the teaching load during the academic year leaves little time for conducting research. However, in either case, robbing Peter to pay Paul can be a problem. The professor at the research university can illegitimately take time from the teaching endeavor to support the research endeavor. The professor at the institution with a focus on teaching can put so much energy into teaching that insufficient time is left for research or creative activity. In either case, the package of obligations is imbalanced.

It may be the case that an institution is out of balance in its allocation of obligations. A new dean may ratchet up the obligation for research productivity—without changing the weighting of other elements in the package of obligations. Or it may be that obligations were not fully understood. For example, during the hiring process both the institution and the professor being hired may have mutually agreed that the job requirements were satisfactory, but either one or both may come to see that the requirements are not being fulfilled as understood. Or it may be that dramatic change refigures obligations. An institution may decide that the next five-year strategic plan should be the catalyst for moving the institution in a very different direction, leaving some long-term employees with a difficult decision about whether to invest significant energies in a new direction that they believe does not comport well with the institution's heritage—or their professional interests.

In cases where institutions undergo significant change, a professor may believe that the contractual obligations under which he or she signed on have been so seriously compromised that little recourse remains other than to seek employment elsewhere. That, however, is a radical decision that may not be feasible from a practical viewpoint. If the tension between institutional change and the package of obligations appears to be an untenable conflict of interest, before making a decision about what recourse to take the professor should first come to terms with issues related to ownership.

That professionals have certain privileges, such as how to structure much of their work, does not provide a license for consistently favoring individual research over other obligations. That fulfilling some professional duties is more satisfying than fulfilling others is not adequate justification for shirking less-than-fulfilling tasks. For example, a professor might find departmental committee work tedious and virtually unproductive, simply a matter of jumping through hoops to affirm the status quo. Thus the professor might opt out of departmental committee work by not attending assigned committee meetings or simply assuming that he or she is not engaged by committee work and will not attend committees even if assigned to him or her. Such an attitude constitutes a failure of collegiality, if not direct insubordination. It fails to engage the full range of activities required of professional educators. Members of the professoriate are obligated to participate in a full-fledged academic life.

We close this chapter by noting that an individual professor's attempt to balance the package of professorial obligations should not be done in isolation from the professor's community of scholars. Above we noted that honestly weighing advice—solicited or unsolicited—is one way to gain wisdom about how to balance responsibilities. We now make a few remarks about the obligation of colleagues to provide advice, even unsolicited advice. As a profession, we may not wish to intrude on our colleagues' freedom to make choices, but such a position becomes unethical when we have good reason to believe that a colleague is using his or her freedom unethically. Aiding and abetting unethical behavior cannot be other than unethical behavior itself. Certainly we should not rush to judgment, but if our concern about a colleague's fulfillment of his or her package of responsibilities appears to have merit, we rightly have the obligation to raise our concern—first privately with the colleague. Then, if the evidence is clear and the colleague intractable, we have a responsibility to pursue our concern with other interested professional parties— other professors in the subdiscipline and discipline, the department chair, and perhaps the dean. Although it is reasonable to expect that concerns would be addressed by other colleagues, such may not be the case; using professional judgment, we have to determine when we have fulfilled our duty to address an ethical lapse. Our hope and belief is that most questionable professorial behavior results from the pressures of making difficult judgments about the allocation of resources under time pressure. Even when undertaken with good intention, one can be unethical in how one resolves conflicts. As a result we also hope that professors will be open to respectful and cordial criticism and suggestions regarding their conduct.

However, knowing that humans tend to have an aversion to being corrected, we recognize that the ethical responsibility to mentor our colleagues (as we would want to be mentored to become more ethical in our teaching) may create long-lasting ill will. Thus we do not recommend ethical mentoring naïvely or casually, but recommend that colleagues use professional judgment to determine how and when to approach a colleague who is struggling to balance his or her package of competing responsibilities.

Conclusion

The following guidelines should be observed to avoid unethical conflicts of interest:

1) In teaching, there is a general obligation to teach courses adequately and to teach as well as possible by devoting time and energy to pedagogical improvement, lesson preparation, feedback, and advice to students.

2) The obligation to teach well can only be overridden by very important and unavoidable conflicting obligations, including obligations to self-care, to family members, and to conduct research or other professional service.

3) Professors should assign materials and design their courses to benefit students rather than to further their own research. Advancement of faculty interests may be a fortuitous additional benefit but not the primary rationale for the structure of courses.

4) To maintain good judgment while determining how to allocate time and plan courses, professors should consult their colleagues to benefit from their experience and perspectives.

4

The Ethics of Classroom Grading

Grading students' performance is a good candidate for the most difficult responsibility a professor has to perform—and one with significant ethical challenges. Finding a professor who has struggled with how to evaluate a particular student's academic efforts would be easy—even finding one who has agonized over the question "B+ or A?" would not be difficult. Although the distinction between a B+ and an A may seem insignificant or trivial, grading is generally a high-stakes issue. As a rule, professors take seriously their grading responsibilities because the stakes *are* so high: graduation, quality of job opportunities, graduate school admission and funding, and various academic honors and awards. As universities are structured today, grading plays a fundamental role in informing and motivating student education, keeping track of student progress within institutions, and evaluating student work for third parties. Indeed, professors legitimately see themselves as gatekeepers who have the responsibility to maintain rigorous disciplinary standards. However one assesses the value of grading, professors have a contractual and professional obligation to grade their students' performance. Grading is an ethical imperative. But what constitutes ethical grading?

To answer that question, we acknowledge that the act of grading is a process that terminates with a grade. Determining whether any particular grade is ethical requires an investigation of the process that yielded the grade. An investigation of the grading process legitimately entails reviewing the relationship between preexisting conditions that have an influence on the classroom and future performance that extends long after the grade has been officially recorded. In other words, students enter a classroom with differing levels of knowledge about the subject for the class, motivation to study the subject, and intellectual aptitude to grasp the subject. In addition, professors enter the classroom with various levels of expertise and longevity as classroom teachers. Ultimately a university education ought to foster the development of students' skills, knowledge base, and habits such that it makes a lasting improvement in their lives and performance. However, while courses should make lasting contributions to student lives, professors must base their grades on what students do during the course. Higher education has no mechanism to revise grades based on future performance outside the classroom—e.g., one cannot revoke degrees in business because the person holding the degrees was convicted of accounting fraud. So although the future can be ignored in making grading recommendations, we will consider the preexisting conditions for effective grading.

In investigating that process, we take it as an ethical principle that a person is not responsible for that which he or she cannot control. In terms of the grading process, this means that professors are not responsible for the ethical dilemmas they inherit, only their responses to them. This principle is vital for any discussion of the ethics of classroom grading because professors inherit dilemmas that have ethical implications for their grading practices. For example, a student may enter a class with inadequate writing skills. Does the professor of political science, for instance, have an obligation to help that student improve his or her writing skills beyond the instruction necessary to produce written work that subscribes to the principles of effective writing in political science?

In providing insight into how one might answer that and other pertinent questions related to the grading process, we investigate the process from the perspective of professional responsibility. Guided by the principle that professors are ethically responsible for what they can control, we divide the grading process into three interrelated parts: preparing to teach, teaching, and grading. We examine the grading process in light of contractual obligations to ground our understanding of duty. At the same time, we appeal to principles of professionalism for interpreting duties stated either explicitly or implicitly in normative contractual obligations.

Pedagogical Preparation and Grading

We begin our discussion of preparing to teach by asserting that preparation for teaching in higher education should include formal training in pedagogy. Our particular concern is formal training in grading, but we see the various elements of teaching as interrelated. (Though there are many terms for it—evaluating, marking, testing, assessing, providing feedback—and significant terminological confusion regarding the topic [Speck & Jones, 1998], we shall use the term *grading* throughout this section.) When people commonly talk about teaching, they refer to what the professor does in the classroom, so the term *teaching* is used in the vernacular to mean "what the professor communicates to students, generally orally." Perhaps this view of teaching is shorthand for everything the professor does before, during, and after class to communicate orally in class, but more likely the part (a professor's communicating orally in class) is taken for the whole, because people who have not taught probably are unaware of what teaching in toto entails. It turns out then that with the discrete tasks that comprise teaching (reading in one's field, structuring a semester and individual class sessions, creating visual aids for classroom use, constructing exercises and examinations of various types, etc.), grading exercises and examinations are assumed either to be part of how professors communicate to students or those individual tasks are not clearly understood in the interlocking relationships that comprise the teaching enterprise. In any case, grading cannot be separated from the requirements of the syllabus, the way daily course content is structured, and the relationship the professor establishes with the students (whether antagonistic or affirming, for example, but see Chapters 5 and 6 for a discussion of professorial conduct regarding students). Professorial teaching responsibilities are a web of tasks; taking a strand from the web weakens it because the strands depend on each other.

In broad terms, preparing to teach includes the preexisting condition of formal preparation to teach, including formal education in grading. However, historically the academy has held that graduate education in a particular subject matter is sufficient preparation for teaching. This is based on an assumption that if a person is successful in learning a particular subject matter during graduate education, the person will possess sufficient knowledge to teach students how to learn—including how to grade students' efforts. In other words, possession of subject matter expertise is sufficient evidence that a person can convey that knowledge to others so that they will have ample opportunity to learn that knowledge.

Implicit in this view is that the ability to perform all the professorial tasks that promote effective student learning (including grading) is somehow acquired by studying a particular subject matter. However, the skills needed for effective teaching are not the skills needed for gaining mastery of a subject matter. For example, Buchen (1998), in reflecting on his initiation into the professorate, notes:

> When I entered the academic profession, I can truthfully say I was not aware of any faculty model to follow. Indeed, spared the requirement of taking methodology courses (a blessing but also a limitation), I did not even have a professional sense of how to structure the transmission of subject matter to students. I was told my knowledge not my methodology was my rock and salvation. As far as putting together a syllabus, the standard advice was to dig out one's old notes or recall the way the course was taught by one of your favorite teachers. Aside from not being the wisest course of action, the other suggestions of colleagues generally were piecemeal Band-Aids. It never occurred to me that matters might be handled any other way than the sink or swim method. Later on when I had to take my turn as department chair and was responsible for "acculturating" new members of the department, I reflected on what would my start have been like if I had a model to follow. What would it have contained? What would it have done for me? Why is a model important at all? (p. 1)

Buchen goes on to say that a model would have helped him "structure my relationships with students" (p. 2), including planning grading that fairly assesses student performance and effectively contributes to the student's education. These two distinctive roles enable the professor to be both advocate and judge, and although the two roles may seem logically necessary ("Who else but the professor should grade his or her students' efforts?"), the two roles are not without potential ethical pitfalls. For example, the two roles should be as clearly delineated as possible so that students are not misled into believing that the advocacy role ("I'm in your corner;

I'm here to help you learn") will undermine the judge role ("I will give you a grade based on the quality of your work, not friendship") or vice versa. Later we will discuss the ethical dilemmas related to these two roles.

We return to Buchen to note that his experience of not being given the tools necessary to teach effectively is not atypical. As Buchen was told regarding pedagogy (and as innumerable Buchens continue to be told), your knowledge—not your methodology—will be your rock and salvation. Huber (1992) satirizes that perspective by noting "teachers are apparently supposed to know how to teach because they have been watching teachers do it since first grade—kind of like learning how to play tennis by sitting in the grandstand" (p. 124). This means that while professors have the duty to provide students with an official performance appraisal in the form of a grade, which has substantial implications for the clients' future, faculty receive little or no formal training in grading effectively, fairly, and accurately.

That professors are not provided with adequate preparation in pedagogy, including solid instruction on grading, is a preexisting condition over which graduate students have little control. So whatever problems in grading result from lack of adequate preparation in pedagogy are not the responsibility of graduate students who are simply following prescribed programs of study leading to credentials for securing tenure-track positions. The ethical responsibility for greater attention to pedagogy lies with graduate programs and the academy more broadly, which have traditionally been resistant to requiring coursework geared toward training graduate students for their future service as faculty members. Even when professors struggle early in their careers as teachers, they may resist consulting literature on grading that could give them guidance, perhaps not even knowing what literature is available. This preexisting condition can have tremendous implications for how professors handle ethical dilemmas in grading.

The Syllabus and the Principle of Specification

In addition to teacher preparation in pedagogy, good grading also requires a basis in a well-planned syllabus. A syllabus can be viewed as a contract between the professor and the students. Students have a right to know what work a course will involve when they sign up for it. Accurate descriptions of assignments and grading standards in the syllabus are required to make student consent to take the course valid.

Of course, some courses may be required and taught by only one professor or in similar manner by several professors, which would make informed consent on the student's part irrelevant. However, there remain other important reasons for thorough disclosure of course requirements in the syllabus. If students are to be graded on the basis of these requirements, fairness requires that they knew of the requirements and had sufficient time to complete them. The spelling out of assignments in the syllabus at the beginning of the course maximizes the fairness of assignments. It also can contribute to teaching effectiveness. Students are likely to get more out of the course if they understand its structure and can effectively plan their own work. Having early guidelines for the selection of a term paper topic not only gives the student a fair chance in succeeding on the assignment, but also makes it more likely that the student will benefit from having a prolonged and coherent research project.

In addition, in our litigious society it is prudent to have as many requirements as possible detailed in writing. Professors defending grades in university appeals boards or in legal courts are on more secure ground the more specific the syllabus. The syllabus has become a document that informs students of various policies, such as academic repercussions for plagiarizing, relationships of unexcused absences to calculation of the course grade, penalties for handing in assignments past the due date, possibilities for extra credit, performance issues related to disabilities, and so forth. Because these policies can have a demonstrable impact on students' grades, students should be made aware of how the professor handles issues that can negatively impact grades. For example, if the professor never announces that after so many absences the student automatically fails the course, the professor cannot ethically fail students for missing a specified number of classes (lacking any other official documents that enunciate such a policy). (Just for clarity, the professor may want to specify in the syllabus what constitutes an absence. Does arriving halfway through the class constitute an absence or a partial absence?) Including such fine details in the syllabus has a tendency to forestall quibbles about how particular policies apply to particular cases. Indeed, if the professor has what might be considered an excessively strict policy, such as allowing no makeups for quizzes regardless of the excuse, then the professor shows prudence by emphasizing during the first class period—and periodically throughout the class—his or her sincerity in following such a policy. The professor may even want to take measures to document students' formal acceptance of the conditions contained in the syllabus, such as having each student sign a statement stating that he or she has read the syllabus and agrees to its conditions.

Professors must exercise judgment to determine what to include, with what degree of detail, in the syllabus. The syllabus is not the course but a roadmap for traveling the course. As a roadmap, the syllabus provides mile markers and landmarks. Not every blade of grass, every shrub, every house, and every person along the way should be included in the syllabus, but the direction the students will trek, the amount of travel time expected each week, the traveler's responsibilities, and the rewards for how well the traveler traverses the terrain should be enunciated.

The syllabus is no trivial endeavor, requiring careful planning to establish clear goals. Let's say, for example, that a history professor says the purpose of his or her course is to teach students to read perceptively or to think critically or to write effectively about history. All well and good, but any of those purposes must be given more specific definition by telling students what type of assignments they should expect, how much they will be *required* to participate in class discussion and activities, what the penalties are for infractions of policies, and what counts for what. Professors' oral responses to students' questions about the syllabus and the class in general are assumed, rightly, to be part of professorial duty during the first day of class. Unless a professor has good pedagogical reasons not to reveal the goals, the structure, and the methods of the course, there appears to be no good reason why students should not be told at the outset (in as much detail as is relevant) how they will be graded.

However, because the syllabus is a roadmap, supplemental materials are necessary during the journey. At the appropriate times while a class progresses, a professor should provide students with more detailed information about particular assignments. Clearly the syllabus does not need to tell students the way points will be calculated for Assignment One. A rubric distributed to students when Assignment One is fully introduced can provide those details. But students should be given concise information in the syllabus that tells them how the professor will grade their efforts.

Note that our focus on specificity regards policy statements, including the grading scale, that will be used for the course. We are not saying that professors cannot enforce expectations that the students either did not consent to or did not read in the syllabus. A professor could require students not to be disruptive in class by not wearing baseball caps and not express that requirement (and consequent penalty) until someone wore a baseball cap. However, the professor could not ethically penalize a student's grade for wearing a baseball cap without giving sufficient warning. If the professor waits to address the penalty for wearing a baseball cap until the first instance of that occurrence, during subsequent classes the professor can penalize students for wearing baseball caps.

The question of whether professors can add and enforce expectations beyond those stated in the syllabus has a two-pronged answer. First, professors may require anything which is logically or practically implied by the syllabus, even if it is not specifically stated. For example, it is assumed that writing assignments (e.g., "a five-page book report") will be completed in the language of course instruction, following its semantic and grammatical rules. Second, anything that reinterprets the policies regarding grading must clearly benefit students so that their opportunities to earn specific grades are not materially changed. If a professor decides during the last three weeks of the class that students have not worked hard enough and assigns a paper, the professor is acting unethically because the students have not been given fair notice of the assignment, which will require a significant investment in student effort (generally a scarce resource), and because the paper will materially change the students' understanding of what was required to earn a final grade for the class. However, it is not unethical for a professor to reduce the workload, perhaps upon judging that time is running short and students have completed sufficient work. Reductions in workload generally do no harm to any individual and therefore are not grounds for complaint. Cancellations of course requirements should generally be done early enough so as not penalize students who have completed the work as initially assigned. The formerly required task can be treated as extra credit or a replacement for another project, such that diligent students still receive some benefit. In principle, professors should give a clear roadmap at the outset of the course and alter the intentions of the syllabus only when unforeseen events require such detours and only if the detours do not burden students unduly by penalizing them for conditions they could not affect.

In principle, the greater the level of *specificity* in the syllabus regarding policies, the better because students are provided with the details they need to determine how they might successfully navigate the course. Our focus on specificity is not merely a matter of practical necessity as students determine how to fit one class schedule and workload into their lives. Foremost our focus on specificity is related to the clarity of the course's aims and objectives, which provide guiding lights for the course's substance. That substance becomes the object of testing and grading; thus, testing and grading take on greater clarity also. We assume that professors seek to give students the greatest possibility for success in a course, and specificity is a powerful tool in communicating what the professor expects from the students for them to earn a particular grade.

The principle of specificity also applies to designing assignments and tests. Again, without belaboring nitty-gritty details, we reiterate the need for clear and precise communication to students about what the professor does and does not expect. For example, a classic question students often ask about a writing assignment is "how many pages do you require?" If the professor has a specific page limit, that limit should be stated in the assignment. If no limit is stated, the professor is saying that the number of pages is not a requirement. The principle of silence also applies to color of paper, font, margins, and any other format or content issues the professor does not specify. It is wise to state even requirements that seem obvious to the professor, as these may be less clear to students lacking academic experience. Professors should strive to make their own expectations on course assignments as explicit as possible. A virtue of the principle of silence is that students begin to cease asking about what is not stated and focus instead on what the assignment specifies.

As a point of clarification, we are *not* saying that it is both necessary and desirable for professors to spell out the rules of grammar just because they will require students to write grammatically correct papers or essay exams. Of course, we enter into a tangled problem when we begin to make assumptions about what students can really be expected to know. The professoriate's widespread disappointment with their students' writing ability suggests that faculty expectations in this area may be too high. Reasonable expectations will vary between courses and institutions. Regardless of the situation, professors should labor to put themselves in the place of their students and ask with them, "What does this professor expect of me if I want a [pick your letter grade] in this class?"

The Purpose of Grading

If assignments and grading standards are to be ethical, professors must plan them with the purposes of grading in mind. Although grading seems like a simple and distinct activity, it involves several different purposes. A grade gives a record of a student's performance that provides an institutional measure of the student's achievement and a ranking of the student's performance vis-à-vis other students. Grades are used to determine student progress within an academic institution and to provide information to third parties who desire to have applicants sorted by their relative abilities. The purpose of ranking students is to determine who has access to other goods—graduation, graduate school, academic honors and awards, and social/economic advancement generally linked with certain employment opportunities.

In any given course some students are likely to outperform others. Assignments can be designed more or less explicitly to separate better and worse students. If all students are getting As, this is normally a sign that grading has been too easy, and that the course will fail to distinguish between students who have done different quality work and have different abilities. On the other hand, if most students are failing, this is a good sign that the course is too difficult and is failing to make qualitative distinctions in student work.

The goal of sorting students does not normally guide the construction and grading of each assignment. However, the fact that course grades will ultimately be used to compile a student's GPA, which in turn partly determines the student's access to other social goods, increases the ethical stakes in all grading. This makes it particularly important that grades accurately reflect student ability so that medical, nursing, law, police, and other programs can select the best applicants. The stakes for students' futures also require that grading be fair, which is to say that equivalent standards are used to assess everyone's work.

It should be noted that the goal of evaluating and sorting students for third parties is not directly beneficial for the student. Of course, if the student excels, the ranking process will be beneficial; but if the student fairs poorly, a rigorous sorting process will be detrimental. However, grading has other purposes more directly beneficial to students.

A second function of grading is to provide students with information about their own performance. This function is partly intertwined with the first: Grades on assessments inform students of where they stand in the class, with its relevance to their GPA and personal advancement. However, grades should also provide students with feedback useful for guiding their future learning. Grades and assessments are not just summative (recording past performance) but also formative, potentially influencing students' performance in the future.

Receiving a letter grade or a numerical score on a paper or test gives students some information about the quality of their work and whether they need to study a certain area in more depth. Such information can be useful if there will be more papers or tests of similar format in the future. However, formative grading does not most commonly or effectively take the form of a letter or numerical grade. A mark such as a C provides the student with very limited information about his or her work. It does not tell the student what was lacking and what was acceptable. Thus it gives the student little guidance but instead notes a general need for improvement.

Formative assessment more commonly takes the form of oral or written narrative feedback from the professor. As a professor walks among students as they are drawing portraits, giving them advice about how to improve their work, he or she is providing formative assessment—no grade is attached to his or her professional judgment at that point. If the goal of education is to help students achieve their greatest potential as learners, formative assessment fits nicely with that goal because students are not formally graded until they have had ample opportunity to respond to professorial judgments to improve their efforts that will be graded.

Indeed, when grading student work, professors do well to think about the goal of providing students with useful feedback. Many critical professorial comments on student written work are designed more to justify the grade that professors give by detailing a paper's imperfections. Though professors probably owe a general rationale for their grades, the number and type of comments should largely be determined by educational aims.

The informational goal of grading, in principle, implies that professors should give students the opportunity to redo assignments. Rewriting a paper or retaking a test would be the most useful way to encourage students to assimilate and apply professorial feedback. If students continue an assignment until they complete it adequately, education is maximized. It could be argued that taken to this extreme, the goal of informing and forming students conflicts with the goal of ranking them. If all were to be enabled to succeed, then there could be no failures. One possible solution would be to only give As to students who succeed the first time, but to allow students to improve low grades through the course.

The major limit to formative assessment is not ethical but practical. The need to teach a certain number of students a certain amount of material limits the amount of feedback and number of learning opportunities that professors can provide. For the professor to give formative feedback to 60 students—in just one class when the professor is teaching other classes as well—does not seem reasonable. Formative feedback is desirable and in the best interests of students, but the professor may not be able to provide adequate formative feedback given the economics of education that demand large sections. Again we come to a situation in which the professor cannot be held responsible for not doing what is educationally advantageous for students because professors have little control over the economic realities of higher education such as class size. This does not mean, of course, that professors are without recourse to their creative powers in solving some of the learning problems that attend large classes (or other educational challenges), but we do stress the ethical implications that attend university education when we know that formative feedback is desirable in enabling students to learn—yet we construct learning environments that severely restrict the use of formative feedback.

A third function of grading stems from the first two: to motivate students to learn. To the extent that students have a stake in grades (or value grades for their own sake) and to the extent that grades signal areas for student improvement, grades can motivate student performance. Indeed, given the current interests, motives, and circumstances of university students, it is difficult to imagine students completing ungraded assignments. The grading of attendance and the prospect of learning material that will help one's grade are the main reasons for students to attend class.

To what extent grades motivate students depends a great deal on a student's attitude about grades, the professor's attitude about grading, and the function of grades in enabling students to learn from a grade. A student's attitude toward grades is most likely linked to his or her educational history. A student who has a record of just passing grades may see grades as a threat to be fended off as best as possible. Another student may be highly motivated and see grades as a challenge to be accepted and mastered; a B is unacceptable and anything less than an A spurns the student on to work harder. A professor's attitude about grading also has an impact on student motivation. If the professor has established a reputation as giving few (if any) As, students may work hard to receive the cherished B, or students may do whatever is minimally necessary to receive a C, believing that the professor's grading standards are unrealistic and impossible. Students who work for a B and those who work for a C are motivated, but the motivations are quite different.

The reliance upon the incentive of good grades and the threat of poor ones to motivate student work is admittedly nonideal. In principle, education should foster not just learning but also the lifelong love of learning. Professors ought to encourage students to inquire into course topics out of intrinsic interest in the pursuit and accumulation of knowledge. Continual emphasis on grades as the bottom line confuses the means with the end: Students learn in order to get good grades, instead of performing well in order to learn. For the time being, most colleges cannot hope to get rid of grading altogether or do away with its use in motivating students. However, it is incumbent on professors to continue to design courses and assignments to engage students. In this way, even if students are initially motivated primarily by grades and advancement toward career goals, they may come to be interested in and value study for its intrinsic good. Also, the motivation provided by grades will only be useful to the extent that the grades and professorial feedback accurately convey useful information to students about their performance and their progress toward achieving course goals.

These three functions of grades—ranking students, giving students formative feedback, and motivating students—work together and against each other. All of the goals generally suggest the importance of accuracy and fairness in grading—grades that objectively reflect students' mastery of material and reflect their performance in relation to other students. In addition to fairness and accuracy, however, considerations of formation and motivation suggest that grading should be evaluated according to its educational effectiveness. Considerations of grading's purposes and the corresponding principles of accuracy, fairness, and effectiveness can be used to assess different grading methods.

Fairness in grading involves giving scores that accurately reflect student performance. However, performance might be measured in different ways. Professors normally attempt to assess the intrinsic quality of student performance, such that the grade reflects their knowledge and ability as manifested in coursework. However, this means that student grades will be heavily influenced by students' prior knowledge and abilities. Students who enter the class with some background in the subject or with more advanced writing and analytic skills will consistently get higher grades. This means that grades do not necessarily measure the effort or amount of learning that students do in a class. Such grades could be argued to be undeserved. By making good grades out of reach for students with poor skills, grading may also be nonideal in terms of motivation and pedagogical effectiveness.

An alternative to measuring the absolute quality of work would be to grade according to individual improvement. To grade on improvement, the professor would have to establish a baseline for each student's learning and then measure how much the student learned in relationship to the baseline. A pretest and posttest could be used to establish a baseline, but the pretest would simply show how much students knew coming into the class; students who knew quite a bit could be disadvantaged because what they would have learned could pale in comparison to what less knowledgeable students could have learned. Unless the baseline could be individualized in some way, which seems an extremely unlikely prospect, student learning would not really be individualized but merely comparative, which would again be ranking via grades. A grading system which emphasized effort and improvement would also be less useful to third parties that want information about students' knowledge and abilities relative to one another.

Grading on the curve suffers from the same problem in a reverse way. What students learn is measured by what the best students learn. If the grades on a particular exercise are not evaluated given a standard established before the grades are given, then students are ranked in relationship to each other, but any student's grade is merely a matter of luck. If Student A is particularly gifted in the subject being studied, then Student A will "set the curve" and other students' learning is graded in relationship to Student A. But students in a different section of the same class could receive higher grades than the comrades of Student A because no Student A "sets the curve" in the other section. Luck should not be the basis of grading, and clearly luck is a prominent feature when professors grade on the curve. One ethical dilemma that attends grading on the curve is that the professor could be compensating for less-than-stellar teaching, and we will discuss this later when we address the problem of the professor being both mentor and judge in the grading process.

Assignment Construction

With these purposes for grading in mind, we turn to the mechanism that frames how a student will be graded—assignments, including examinations. We have already noted that clear, complete assignments are necessary adjuncts to the syllabus, but determining what exactly needs to be communicated to students for them to have all the information necessary to execute an assignment successfully is a more demanding task than it may appear. But not to construct effective assignments certainly has ethical dimensions, as Hobson (1998) notes when he says "lackluster assignment construction contributes greatly to students' difficulties in completing assignments to their own satisfaction and that of their professors. Assignment construction also affects grading ease and reliability" (p. 52). Hobson makes two important points. First, the quality of the assignment can have a negative impact on the quality of students' efforts to satisfy the assignment. In effect, poor quality assignments can contribute to poor quality work. If a professor is not cognizant of how to construct and evaluate the instructions that constitute an assignment, the professor may be evaluating students' work unfairly—assuming that the assignment was crystal clear and students simply failed to understand what the professor required. Students are seen as having comprehension problems when, in truth, the professor's assignment was murky. Second, Hobson notes that the brunt of "lackluster assignment construction" is borne by students when professors evaluate students' work in relationship to the assignment and find the work wanting. If students do not know what the criteria are, then meeting them is a matter of luck in guessing what the professor wanted. Fairness in grading involves the idea that grades match knowledge, ability, or learning—and are not according to luck. Imprecise assignments lead not only to guesswork on students' part, but also to inconsistent standards when professors are grading. When students answer questions in different ways due to a lack of clarity, professors are more likely to develop evolving, and thus unreliable, standards in the course of grading. Our purpose here is not to provide extensive details about assignment construction; literature on how to evaluate various assignments is available (Anderson & Speck, 1998; Angelo & Cross, 1993; Banta, Lund, Black, & Oblander, 1996, pp. 276–295; Davis, 1993, pp. 239–311; Speck, 1998, 2000, 2002). Our point is that the requirements of assignments should be communicated clearly and concisely to increase students' likelihood and equality of opportunity for success.

Tests of various types represent a different challenge, although not entirely divorced from the challenges that attend assignment construction. Assignment construction has not been given the scrutiny that has been focused on testing instruments. An entire industry represented by standard achievement tests has evolved based on classic testing theory, which defines what constitutes reliability and validity in testing. We will focus on validity, in part, because classroom grading has generally not been much concerned about measuring a student's performance over time using the *same* assessment instrument. In strict terms, reliability entails using the same instrument over time and comparing a student's scores on the several testing occasions. However, as Shale (1996) points out, reliability can be considerably more sophisticated:

> Reliability in multiple-choice testing is a matter of assessing the consistency of results over a period of time (which is a measure of the stability of scores) and over different forms of the instrument (which is a measure of equivalence) and of assessing consistency within the instrument itself (internal consistency). (p. 77)

Clearly the technical language used to discuss reliability is unfamiliar to most academics. It is also difficult to test because it requires comparing responses to the same questions over time. Professors normally don't have time to retest their students on a given subject. Reusing test questions in different classes from term to term also risks students gaining access to questions in advance of the exam, making test results inaccurate and unfair.

Professors may opt to use professionally designed tests under the assumption that such tests have a seal of approval from testing experts, but the questions from such tests may be trivial (a recitation of mere facts, such as dates and names) and not match the learning that takes place in a local classroom. Thus tests that have been standardized for reliability tend to be invalid. It appears, therefore, that the canons of classical testing theory may not have high applicability to classroom-constructed tests. (After discussing essay questions below, we will recommend ways professors might construct tests that meet their classroom needs.)

Furthermore, it is not clear to what extent reliability should be a goal of testing. On one hand, if a test yields consistent results from term to term, this suggests a lack of arbitrariness and thus fairness. However, the norm of repeatability assumes that students should do equally well from term to term, which does not seem to take into account that classes can vary in ability. Moreover, if improvement in teaching is possible, then test scores themselves should improve. It appears, therefore, that reliability is not a good match for determining fairness in classroom grading.

Validity, however, is a major concern for classroom grading. According to classic testing theory, validity means that a testing instrument measures whatever it purports to measure. For example, here is a threat to validity: Professor P uses essay exams to grade students' learning. However, at times Professor P has trouble reading certain students' writing. Is Professor P grading students on their learning or the legibility of their writing? Indeed,

Professor P is sometimes perplexed by Student S's essay responses because Professor P perceives Student S to be quite articulate in the classroom but Student S's essay responses compare unfavorably to Student S's oral classroom participation. Taking into account Student S's classroom participation, Professor P gives a sympathetic reading (and sympathetic grade) to Student S. Is Professor P grading Student S on her answers to the essay exam or on her classroom participation or both? It appears that two variables are confounded in Professor P's grading of Student S.

A test must satisfy certain conditions to be valid. The questions must measure what the questions purport to measure; in the case of multiple choice tests, for example, *the* answer must beat out competing answers by demonstrating that it is valid in relation to the question being asked. We should note that classic testing theory is based on statistical principles, and as Scharton (1996) points out, validity is a complex concept that entails construct, content, concurrent, and predictive validity (p. 55).

Essay questions (also called writing prompts), yet another common form of classroom testing, also require careful construction. Much of the literature on writing prompts addresses large-scale essay testing, such as the essay portion of standardized tests (Brossell, 1983; Brown, Hilgers, & Marsella, 1991; Hoetker & Brossell, 1989; Hult, 1987; Powers, Fowles, Farnum, & Gerritz, 1992; Ruth & Murphy, 1998; White, 1988). Research that evaluates the effectiveness of prompts vis-à-vis the scoring of students' essays written in response to the prompts can be helpful in providing professors with insights into how to construct effective prompts (Baker, 1982; Carlman, 1986; Hoetker, 1982; Hult, 1987; O'Donnell, 1984). Asking students, "What were the major causes of World War I?" is merely a listing exercise that requires students to provide answers that are easily accessible. However, asking students to explain the role of anarchists in the outbreak of World War I by providing a brief history of anarchism immediately prior to World War I and relating the anarchists' concerns to at least two other social movements that helped provoke World War I is a synthetic exercise that requires students to draw upon one possible cause of the war and relate that cause to other causes so as to show possible relationships.

Murphy and Ruth (1993) and Ruth and Murphy (1984) discuss the problem of how students read essay prompts. Indeed, Scharton (1989) found that educators and students can have very different interpretations of a prompt, which "may affect the results of evaluation" (p. 179). Greenberg (1992) confirms that observation by noting, "Students' interpretations of the directions and the details of writing assignments may differ drastically from the interpretation of the teacher who wrote the assignment" (p. 12). In fact, Dudley-Evans (1988) shows that the word *discuss*, a word used commonly in prompts, can have several different meanings. If how to read a prompt is a problem, that problem is intensified by the way prompts are constructed. Brand (1992) says, "Over the long haul effective essay questions are simply basic to effective essay answers" (p. 172), a conclusion also reached by O'Donnell (1984, p. 243). Thus a prompt that makes clear its demands elicits better responses from students, and a better comparison of their knowledge, than a prompt that makes its demands less clear (Kinzer, 1987).

The authors we have cited raise important issues about writing prompts that have ethical import because any ineptitude that influences the creation of effective writing prompts can have a deleterious effect on how students respond to the prompt *and* how those responses are graded. In such a case, who is culpable? The answer is that the professor—because of lack of expertise in writing effective prompts—is culpable, even if no malicious intent is present. Yet students take the brunt of the error. Brand (1992), however, sounds a note of hope by saying that "faculty at every level in every discipline can become careful and graceful authors of essay questions" (p. 171). How does that happen?

Professors have a responsibility to test what has been taught to determine what has been learned, whether using a test, writing prompt, or any other evaluative mechanism. This means that the professor must be able to articulate clearly what has been taught. If a professor cannot say with certainty that he or she taught students how to interpret the major themes in Shakespeare's tragedies, how to dissect a frog, or how to analyze an argument to determine whether a speaker has provided sufficient evidence, then what is being graded is vague and students cannot know what to expect from the professor's evaluation of their work. Once the professor can clearly articulate what was taught with a level of specificity that makes concrete what was expected of students, the professor should determine what type of testing instrument is the best to measure what students learned.

Subjectivity and Objectivity in Grading

Tests, prompts, and scoring guides that measure artistic or speaking skills can be evaluated on a continuum with subjectivity and objectivity as the endpoints. An objective assessment is one that can be scored on the basis of factual accuracy. A subjective assessment is one whose evaluation is not simply a matter of assessing facts but requires judgment. In an objective test, each question has one more-or-less unquestionably correct answer. A student's score on an objective test can be calculated by totaling the number of correct answers. Because there is little room for judgment, objective tests allow for consistency, and thus fairness, in grading. Fatigue or halo effects are not likely to bias scoring as the professor moves through an objective test.

The drawbacks of objective tests—which usually take multiple choice, true/false format—are that they may not be valid measures of a student's understanding of course material, including the ability to synthesize and apply concepts. Objective tests, in order to eliminate judgment, do not allow for individual student expression in their responses. They test students' ability to recognize correct answers but not the ability to integrate class material into their own thinking.

If objectivity refers to absence of judgment in the grading process, then there are no strictly objective tests. Professorial judgment is needed to determine which questions are appropriate measures of student knowledge. What grading scale to use is also a matter of judgment. Objective tests classically have assigned grades according to the percent correct following a fixed scheme (e.g., 90+ is an A, 80 to 89 a B, etc.), but these scales themselves are not objectively based. To say that a student must know 90% of material rather than 70% to have mastery is a matter of judgment regarding the definition of mastery or excellence. What correct percentage constitutes excellence and adequacy depends upon the difficulty of the questions and material. For this reason, the givers of objective tests frequently end up incorporating elements of the curve, with its relational grading, to determine baseline expectations.

Subjective assessments—normally essays, projects, and other written or oral work—require individual responses to and synthesis of course material. Professors must evaluate not only student knowledge of facts but also student ability to relate facts. The way students express themselves will influence the way the professor reads students' answers to the question, and matters of taste—including style, diction, grammatical constructions, and so forth—are not easily disentangled from the content of students' responses.

Grading that requires judgment is frequently accused of being arbitrary. But even the grading of subjective assessments is not without objective elements. First, subjective assessments (such as a paper in the humanities or social sciences) generally contain objective elements (such as the assertion of facts and implementation of logical reasoning) that can be evaluated more-or-less definitively. Professors' judgment of students' synthetic, individualized expression also has some objective basis. Essay graders judge things such as relevance, creativity and originality, cogency, and clarity. Though these do not lend themselves to direct empirical testing or quantification, no knowledgeable reader or writer doubts that they are valid criteria that essays satisfy to varying degrees. Similarly, while one might question the precision with which art can be judged, art professors can generally distinguish between better crafted, more inspired, and less inspired student work. Our concern is not to outline all the criteria by which essays and art can be judged. Rather it is to make the point that even subjective assessments have objectively defensible bases.

Although subjective assessments contain objective elements, the greater amount of professorial judgment, the greater the room for bias and inconsistency in grading. It is widely recognized that knowledge of a student's name affects the essay grades that professors give. Other factors that have little to do with the quality of work may also affect the grading of subjective assessments—the quality of print, whether the professor shares the student's view, and the mood of the instructor. According to the well-documented halo effect, essays graded after a really good essay will tend to be given a higher score, since the A will have become the baseline grade in the professor's mind. Professors may either lower or increase expectations as they read student work, giving the location of the student's paper in the grading pile an indefensible impact on grading.

However, through precaution and diligence these problems can be minimized. Professors can have students turn in their papers with codes instead of names. They can also reread earlier papers after reading all papers, to make sure that a relatively consistent standard was employed throughout. Subjective assessments inevitably involve more fallibility and thus risk of unfairness and inconsistency. However, at the same time they retain advantages over multiple choice tests insofar as they likely have more validity in measuring the whole range of skills and understanding that professors want students to learn.

Teaching

The literature on effective teaching in higher education is substantial (Andrews, Garrison, & Magnusson, 1996; Baiocco & DeWaters, 1998; Bess, 1982; Brookfield, 1991; Brown & Atkins, 1988; Chickering & Gamson, 1987; Eble, 1990; Ericksen, 1984; Feldman, 1988; Findley, 1995; Menges, Weimer, & Associates, 1996; Roth, 1997; Svinicki & Menges, 1996). Our purpose here, however, is not to review that literature. Rather our purpose is to explore alignment among teaching, learning, and grading because (as we have already averred) grading cannot be abstracted from the classroom enterprise.

We focus on the alignment issue, taking a pragmatic cue from Davis (1993) when she notes:

> Students study in ways that reflect how they think they will be tested [and thus graded]. If they expect an exam focused on facts, they will memorize details; if they expect a test that will require problem solving or integrating knowledge, they will work toward understanding and applying information. (p. 239)

We assert that the professor has an obligation to ensure that how the class content is delivered fits with student expectations about what should be learned and how that learning will be tested and graded.

Let's take the lecture method as an example of alignment. The central purpose of a lecture is to deliver a specific body of information. Lectures can be, and often are, augmented in various ways—handouts, PowerPoint presentations, pauses for questions and responses, and interactive activities that engage students in the learning process. But the lecture proper is a method for providing students with a specific body of information. In the literature on student learning, lectures are classified as examples of passive learning because the activities students are engaged in during a lecture—listening, taking notes, trying to process information—are relatively passive compared to other teaching tools, such as small-group work that, when structured effectively, requires students to interact with each other productively regarding the topic at hand.

A limitation of the lecture method, as O'Donnell and Dansereau (1994) point out, is that it does not allow students to encode information in long-term memory by rehearsing, reorganizing, and elaborating on the information:

> A typical undergraduate rarely has the opportunity to engage in these encoding processes during a lecture. When students take notes, the notes are likely to be incomplete and contain errors. Encoding of information is likely to be impoverished, and a reliance on inadequate notes for review is likely to compound students' difficulties. (p. 117)

Knowing the limitations of the lecture method, professors will want to evaluate their testing methods to ensure that they are not assuming students can adequately rehearse, reorganize, and elaborate information from the lectures. For example, if a professor delivers a lecture and expects students to synthesize relationships noted in the lecture on an examination without providing students with the tools necessary to make those connections, the professor is misaligning the instruction method with the testing method and creating ethical grading problems.

Of course, a professor could object to our criticism of misalignment by appealing to what students ought to know. "Students ought to know how to synthesize information," an interlocutor might reply, "so it is perfectly appropriate for a professor to assume that students can synthesize information delivered in a lecture and use their skills at synthesis when answering test questions about the material delivered via the lecture."

We believe alignment is the answer to such an objection. In important ways, professorial attitudes about teaching are a central concern related to the success of the alignment of the teaching-learning-grading transaction. For example, Baiocco and DeWaters (1998), in their study of distinguished professors in higher education, found that these professors "looked internally when there was a problem with students learning; instead of blaming the students for not learning, they attempted to identify the teaching problem" (p. 132). Thus those professors operated on the principle that teaching had a direct impact on learning and if students were experiencing difficulties in learning, the first avenue of recourse was to reevaluate teaching effectiveness. Ownership of responsibility for teaching as a method for learning, not merely a way to transfer knowledge, is crucial to any exploration of the teaching-learning-grading enterprise. Such ownership bears emphasis because as Anderson (1989) stated, professors "are often unreceptive to the idea of adapting courses to the developmental needs of their students" (p. 101). Andrews, Garrison, and Magnusson (1996) substantiate that observation by asserting "institutions of higher education tend to be content driven, and students are expected to have the metacognitive motivation and strategies to direct and manage their learning" (p. 83). However, teaching (by its very nature) is an activity based on relationships conducive to helping students learn. A professor who operates under the assumption that the professor's role is merely to teach and the students' role is to learn cuts the nerve of effective teaching and raises questions about ethical conduct as an educator. Professors should test their assumptions about student learning, and when those assumptions prove to be false given student performance, professors should 1) not penalize students unduly and 2) correct their teaching and testing methods to enable students to perform well—to learn, for example, how to synthesize.

In using lecture as an example of alignment, we are not making a value judgment about the use of lectures as a legitimate teaching tool. We are, however, raising ethical concerns related to the alignment of teaching, learning, and grading. Clearly, to teach in a way that is incommensurate with the way students are tested and graded is an ethical issue that not only should be of concern to professors, but also a matter of vigilance as professors evaluate and recalibrate teaching and testing methods in relationship to student learning. As Hutchings (1996) notes:

Putting the emphasis on learning mitigates otherwise divisive debates about the "best" teaching methods, where the advocates of, say, cooperative learning line up on one side of the room and the devotees of lecture on the other, pointing fingers at each other. Shifting attention from how teachers teach to what (and how well) students learn makes for more constructive debate and problem solving. (p. 37)

Grading

Up to this point we have alluded to the elephant sitting in the middle of the classroom, but when we discuss grading we note that the most significant ethical dilemma that attends classroom grading is the conflict between the professor's role as mentor and judge. Professors plan the course and give instruction in order to help students, but at the same time they evaluate how much students have learned.

Because professors are simultaneously the legislators, adjudicators, and executors of classroom rules (including grading policy) this places a great deal of authority in the professor's hands. Most institutions of higher education have a grade appeal process, but unless the professor has acted in a capricious and arbitrary manner, students have little hope of being heard with a sympathetic ear. The balance of power in the classroom tilts heavily toward professors, and because of that, professors have a significant ethical obligation to ensure that they are not abusing their authority to harm students and diminish students' opportunities to learn.

Because professors both teach and grade the results of their teaching, they have a stake in the grades they give. The grades students receive are supposed to reflect learning; thus, in principle, grades reflect how well the course was taught, higher grades reflecting better teaching. So professors are grading themselves and have an incentive to inflate grades. Consider, for example, a professor on the tenure-track who teaches at an institution where teaching is the primary mission. Student evaluations are used to judge teaching effectiveness. When the professor grades students, he or she tends to give higher grades because higher grades lead to happier students and, concomitantly, higher student evaluations. In turn, higher student evaluations lead to tenure and increased salary. Giving a higher grade than a student deserves also can fend off unpleasant encounters with angry and upset students who otherwise would want to know why they didn't receive a higher grade. In short, every grading act involves a choice between the incentive to give an easy grade and the duties of integrity and fairness in giving accurate grades. This means that grading one's own courses involves a kind of conflict of interest.

Professors also can use grades to punish students they don't like (or reward those they do). And who would know whether the professor engineered an assignment to punish a class or happened not to "catch" points that would be deducted from a student's score because the student appears to be working hard or is particularly attractive? Where are the controls that give integrity to grading?

To address the ethical dilemmas arising from professorial grading authority, some have advocated external evaluators who have access to grading criteria but are not part of the teaching effort (Sawyer, 1975, 1976) or cross-evaluation in which professors exchange their grading responsibilities (Raymond, 1976; Tritt, 1983), especially for student performance in writing. This would take away incentives toward grade inflation or the prospect of penalizing students for their conduct in class. Others recommend that students participate in various ways in the grading process, including helping to create grading standards and completing self-assessments (Johnston, 1987; Kirby, 1987; McNamara & Deane, 1995) that are averaged into the final grade.

The practicality of external and cross-evaluators is not very great. It would require extensive coordination between faculty familiar with each others' course material and course plans. Since professors know each other and, at least within the same major, know many of the same students, it is unclear whether noninstructor graders would solve problems of conflicts of interest and bias. Student participation in the grading process certainly has merit in that it provides students with opportunities to learn more about the complexities of grading and to practice evaluation skills that almost certainly will come in handy when students embark on their careers and take on managerial responsibilities. However, student grading—with its lack of expertise—is open to a problematic lack of consistency, fairness, and validity.

Another way to address possible biases in grading is to use blind grading. Students identify themselves by using a random number that only they know, and the professor uses that number to identify student work. This approach may not be possible when members of a small class work on clearly identifiable projects.

Ultimately ethical grading does depend on the personal integrity of the professor. We can attempt to create firewalls that separate the authority to teach from the authority to grade, and to the extent that firewalls (such as blind grading) are effective, they can lend credence to claims that the professor is attempting to grade fairly. All that we have said in this chapter points toward open communication, clear guidelines, explicit instructions, and alignment of the multifarious tasks that comprise the teaching-learning-grading enterprise as the best approach to ethical grading. If our arguments about the indivisibility of the teaching-learning-grading enterprise are cogent, then assigning a grade will logically follow, so at this point we simply reaffirm that the process of grading terminates with a grade, and assigning ethical grades is authenticated by using an ethical process in preparing to teach and in teaching.

Assigning a grade is but a part of a long, interlinked process that includes a variety of ethical issues—and potential ethical pitfalls. The complexities of the grading process cannot be reduced to surefire answers. However, the principles of ethical decision-making derived from contractual obligations, professional standards, and normative moral principles provide an adequate foundation for constructing and delivering course content in ways that are aligned with grading student learning. The more that foundation can be built upon when professors engage in decision-making regarding the grading process, the more probable that professorial decisions will be ethically defensible.

Conclusion

Our discussion of ethical considerations in grading suggests that professors observe the following considerations in grading:

1) Professors should plan assignments and grading to attain the three purposes of grades by:
   - Accurately evaluating and ranking students to provide information to third parties
   - Providing students useful information about their own progress
   - Motivating study and learning

2) Two ethical principles are central in guiding grading:
   - Effectiveness (assignments should be constructed and feedback tailored in a way that enhances learning)
   - Fairness, which entails at least:
     - ~ Validity (grades given should accurately reflect student's level of mastery of the course goals)
     - ~ Consistency (grade should result from a consistent procedure and standard, applied equally to all students)

3) Good assignment construction and grading practice also includes:
   - Specificity (assignments clearly and precisely specify what students are expected to do)
   - Alignment (assignments and grading should focus on material studied and vice versa)

5

Professional Conduct: Respect and Offense in Teaching

Can there be any doubt that professors should treat students with respect? To ask the question is to answer it. In fact, we have not found a scholarly book or article that endorses professorial disrespect for students. Yet determining what constitutes respect, and what constitutes a violation of respect, is challenging. To meet this challenge we propose that both respect and disrespect can be measured by appealing to a universal concept of personhood that states human beings are to be treated with dignity because they are human beings. In addition, we appeal to the principle that anyone who wields authority over another person has an ethical duty to use that authority so that the dignity of personhood is not diminished. In effect, we are advocating both a general principle of respect for all human relationships and a specific principle of respect for relationships when one person has legitimate authority over another. Our particular concern is professorial authority over students as it relates to professorial conduct regarding students. Our discussion of professorial conduct will provide an analysis of what constitutes respect, examine forms of disrespect, offer reasons why professors might disrespect students, and conclude by affirming that disrespect to students is unethical and has no place in the academy.

An Examination of Respect

Because *dis*respect is the negation of respect, we begin by defining respect. Instead of appealing to a dictionary definition, we think we can parse the term by appealing to three common perceptions of respect. First, to respect someone means to hold him or her in high regard. Thus when a person says, "I really respect her for the way she handled that situation," the speaker is saying the person he or she respects deserves admiration and has acted in a commendable manner. It is important to note that this use of respect is based upon actions. According to this merit-based understanding of respect, a person earns respect; thus the merit-based approach requires an act that deserves respect. Such an approach to respecting students would mean that when a student has demonstrated that he or she has earned respect, then the professor will respect the student. Indeed, some professors may embrace wholly the merit-based approach to respecting students and devote themselves to the most worthy students. Grading is a form of acknowledgement accorded by performance and thus fits the pattern of merit-based respect. Students are given positive feedback from the professor because of intelligent papers and class discussion, diligent work, and enthusiasm for the subject matter. On the other hand, students who perform poorly, put in little effort, and rarely come to class earn no merit-based respect. They not only earn poor grades but are likely to lose the professor's esteem and receive condemnation. As discussed in Chapter 4, assigning marks based on merit is itself a challenging task.

A second perception of respect is based on status and role relationships, as in "Citizens should respect their leaders" or "Children should respect their parents." The import of this understanding of respect is that by virtue of a person's office or title respect is due to the person. This use of respect may or may not carry with it the notion of admiration. A student can respect a professor without admiring him or her, thus respecting the office without holding the officeholder in the highest regard. That is, this status-based understanding of respect does not entail that the one being respected do anything meriting admiration. Of course, as we have framed status-based respect it is formal, but in reality merit-based respect is neither far behind nor far ahead of status-based respect. For instance, the manner in which a professor fulfills his or her official duties can either enhance or limit the level of formal respect students give to the professor. In other words, formal status-based respect adheres to an office or title, but such formal respect is either affirmed or devalued given the acts of the person. Indeed, disrespect for improper, unethical, or illegal acts a person perpetrates while holding such a position is magnified because the position is honorific, bestowing particular responsibilities. Students are owed respect, in part, because of their role in relationship to the professor. By taking on the role of professor in relationship to students, professors acquire a responsibility to treat students with general care and respect regardless of their accomplishments. Student status thus merits some respect from professors. An inattentive or abusive husband deserves greater censure than an inattentive or abusive boyfriend, all things being equal, because the formal title husband carries with it greater responsibilities than that of boyfriend.

A third form of respect is that which is owed to all individuals based upon their nature as persons—nature-based respect. This intrinsic respect for humanity can be defended in various ways. Under a theological paradigm, human beings are accorded respect by their divine creator and universal legislator. Other philosophical approaches define "personhood" in terms of the capacity for reason, moral agency, or experiences of pleasure and pain. Thus respect is owed to any who meet these basic thresholds of moral worth. Regardless which view is taken, ethicists widely agree that human beings have features which demand moral concern and dignified treatment. As with status-based respect, students thus merit respect as persons, independently of their particular achievements.

The merit-, status-, and nature-based approaches to respect are not mutually exclusive. The person who said, "I really respect her for the way she handled that situation," could add, "and that's the way a supervisor should act," demonstrating that status-based expectations are at work in evaluating merit-based respect. Or the person could add, "and that's the way one person ought to treat another," revealing that merit-based praise is supported by a nature-based paradigm.

For our purposes, we advocate a blend of the three approaches that says, "Professors should treat students with respect because as humans (nature-based respect) and students (status-based respect) they have a right to be respected. However, students can earn merit-based respect depending on their ability to satisfy academic requirements."

What we have done so far is categorize respect so that the respect that comes from personhood and student status is delineated from earned respect. However, the contrast between merit-based respect and status- and nature-based respect requires explication, particularly because lapses in performance can have a profound effect on the standing of status- and nature-based respect.

We acknowledge that in extreme cases one's personhood (nature-based respect) can be diminished because of the gravity of a person's actions. The classic example of this is Hitler. Because of the enormity of his transgressions, people commonly refer to his personhood with disrespect: He's a monster, a devil, not human. Our purpose in using Hitler as an example of someone who appears to have lost personhood respect because of his actions is not to debate whether Hitler did indeed lose in some way personhood respect. However, in using Hitler as an example of potential loss of personhood respect, we note that such a loss would require enormously outrageous acts and is therefore atypical. In the classroom setting, the loss of personhood respect is quite remote and so exceptional that we affirm the necessity of professors' maintaining personhood respect even in the face of lapses that legitimately reduce merit-based respect.

Take, for example, a student who has been proved guilty of plagiarism, one of the most common and widely condemned academic crimes. In terms of merit-based respect, the professor is obligated to inform the student who plagiarizes that his or her actions regarding plagiarism deserve censure. Indeed, the student's status as a student may be in jeopardy if the prosecution of the proved plagiarism can result in suspension from school or dismissal from an academic program. But what about the student's standing regarding nature-based or personhood respect? Plagiarism, because it is a form of theft, does bring shame on the student's personhood, and the student rightly loses respect for a shameful act. The loss of merit-based respect and the consequences of that loss regarding how the student's character is viewed, however, do not entail the professor treating the student with disrespect, for the loss of respect and being treated with disrespect are distinct. The professor may, indeed, have less respect for the student's character but still treat the student with dignity, demonstrating disapproval of the student's behavior. The professor can say to the student, "You have violated a code of academic behavior that rightfully requires a penalty, which I will administer, but my hope is that the penalty will be a catalyst for you to understand the gravity of your violation and to change your behavior in the future so that you will subscribe willingly to the code of academic behavior." The tone, demeanor, and attitude in which such a message is delivered can say much about the professor's intention to treat the student with dignity while prosecuting the case against the student. In fact, the very process of holding an individual accountable for his or her actions accords an individual respect as a moral agent with the capacity to distinguish between right and wrong.

A number of complex factors can cause students to fail in the classroom. Poor performance does not necessarily result exclusively from the lack of either effort or intellectual capacity for which students are thought to be directly responsible. Students' failure to attend class, maintain attention, and complete assignments effectively is frequently caused in part by things such as their academic background, predilections, economic status, or familial responsibilities—which are not under the student's control. If a student, for example, is working to support a family while attending college, the energies the student can devote to his or her education are delimited by other obligations. Such a student may be devoting the appropriate time and effort, given his or her other duties, to academic work and still not be able to achieve more than passing grades. Such a student—and many nontraditional students fit this example— deserves respect, even merit-based respect, because he or she is achieving a level of success commensurate with his or her circumstances. This example does not provide all the data points necessary to determine whether the student is making a good-faith effort, but this is precisely the situation most professors encounter because rarely do they have access to all the data points in a particular student's life to make an unambiguous judgment about the why of student performance. Thus student merit should not be the sole basis for faculty recognition and respect.

Indeed, the screw turns both ways; heaping on respect because of a student's success under the merit-based approach can suffer from the same problem of missing data points, and even give credit for privilege (the status-based approach) without regard to issues related to nature-based respect (personhood). Does a professor really want to praise an academically gifted student who is overbearing, vindictive, and inhospitable to others? According to our notion, the professor should separate merit-based and personhood respect, saying to the student, "You're showing a good understanding of the subject in this course, and you rightly earned an 'A' on this assignment, but I'd like you to be more respectful of your classmates." In other words, personhood respect is due to the disrespectful, even when the disrespectful do not respond respectfully to the personhood respect they are given. This does not mean that students who continue to show disrespect after being clearly informed of the problems their disrespect is causing should not be punished. Indeed, if professors allow a student's disrespect to continue, they are culpable. Our purpose here is not to digress by discussing issues related to addressing student classroom misconduct, but we point to advice on how to address such misconduct (Amada, 1999).

Thus far, we have established that respect can be seen as three often-overlapping categories—merit-, status-, and nature-based respect. Professors have an obligation to treat students with respect without any prior knowledge of students' behavior because of students' status as students and because of students' personhood. Students' performance will directly affect the level of merit-based respect professors should give, and depending upon the nature of that performance, students' performance may call into question professorial regard for a student's status- and nature-based respect. However, disrespect in terms of disrespectful treatment is an inappropriate response to a student's loss of respect. Rather, professors should treat a student's loss of respect with dignity because students continue to have status as learners, and the hope for remediation should be prominent in attempts to regain respect. In addition, students maintain personhood that requires respect.

Respect in Treatment and Attitude

We have distinguished between three different grounds for respecting students. There is another type of ambiguity in thinking about how students are owed respect. Respect is both a positive psychological attitude that one can take toward other people and a manner of treating people appropriately. The most basic requirement for professors is to treat students with the respect merited by their accomplishments, status, and personhood. If professors treat students well in general and as they deserve to be treated in particular instances, they follow their duties regarding respecting students.

Professors (like others) are responsible for how they treat others, not how they think about them; viewing others with respect is not obligatory. A misanthropic curmudgeon who doesn't think well of his or her students or colleagues may nonetheless treat them decently and fairly and thereby satisfy his or her professional requirements. First, individuals have relatively little control over how they think about others. While individuals can refrain from acting on negative thoughts about others, it isn't clear to what extent they can choose to refrain from having negative thoughts. Second, psychological attitudes are not susceptible to outside regulation and enforcement, since we cannot read each others' minds.

However, it would be preferred if professors cultivated respectful attitudes as well as behavior toward students. First, although psychological respect is not necessary for respectful treatment, it makes it much more likely. Thus, if professors can cultivate esteem for students as persons who are facing various challenges and have potential for achievement, they are more likely to treat students with care, concern, and dignity. Disgust with students' limitations, mistakes, lack of work ethic, lack of interest, ignorance, or misconduct is likely to show in professors' words, tone, and manner of addressing students.

If professors display lack of respect for students' status and personhood, they risk injuring the student psychologically. Although we are encouraged from an early age to think that names—insults and denigration—do not hurt, it is plain that they do. Denigration can be particularly harmful when it comes from an authority figure, such as an educator. For this reason, educators have a responsibility to avoid treating students as lacking moral worth and cognitive ability. Not only are such insults painful, but they may also become self-fulfilling. If students are told by their professors (as well as by parents or other authorities) that they are dumb, incompetent, or irredeemably morally impaired, students may give up and accept such labels. For this reason it remains important for professors to retain role and personhood respect for students even when they can legitimately give a student poor marks for merit. The tendency of psychological attitudes to spill over into behavior gives a strong reason for professors to attempt to cultivate basic respect for students, as individuals with both feelings and potential, regardless of their current level of achievement.

Separate from its effect on students, it is also ideal for professors as individuals to cultivate respect for students. If personhood and student-status merit respect, then as lovers of the truth professors ought to recognize these basic values. Furthermore, recognizing and appreciating the dignity of their students would make the teaching profession more fulfilling. It is common for instructors to spend much of their time lamenting the subpar performance of most students and wistfully remembering the accomplishments of a handful of exceptional students. Such an attitude leads professors to view themselves as wasting most of their teaching time. However, to the extent that professors are able to appreciate the humanity of all of their students, their everyday courses and interactions with students acquire more importance. Professors can find a sense of purpose in their role of assisting students to merely acceptable levels of academic achievement if they appreciate students' challenges, are concerned about students' well-being, and have hope for the students' continued progress.

Disrespectful Speech and Behavior: Offense and Denigration

To this point we have only given the most general description of what treating students with respect as client/wards and persons involves. We have only been able to refer generally to an obligation to treat students with care, dignity, and decency. Greater specification of what this involves is achieved by demarcating some forms of treatment that do and do not constitute disrespect for the student.

The most clear cases of disrespect were alluded to earlier. These are cases in which the professor directly denies the personhood or membership status to the student. If the professor does not grade a student fairly or give the student equal opportunities in terms of assignment completion and assistance with the course, the professor fails to honor his or her obligations to the student as a member of the class. A physical assault constitutes disrespect for the personhood of the other individual, denying the basic concern for the well-being and suffering of another individual. As we mentioned earlier, verbal assaults can also constitute disrespect of personhood. If a professor directly denies a student's moral or intellectual humanity—such as by saying "You're an idiot" or "You'll never amount to anything"—the professor not only fails to acknowledge the student's personhood but directly assaults it. Such denigration is incompatible with respectful treatment. By refusing to show concern for the student or take him or her seriously as an intelligent individual, the professor also denies full class membership to the student and thus violates professional role responsibilities.

If direct insults to students are clear cases of disrespect, more difficult cases arise in which students are offended by things faculty say or do. Giving offense is a clear candidate for disrespect. Yet to offend someone is not necessarily to disrespect him or her. An individual may feel offense when confronted with any statement or action that he or she finds surprising, disagreeable, or unpleasant. The offending act need not deny or denigrate personhood or be meant as an assault upon moral or intellectual status; professors do not necessarily have an obligation to avoid giving offense to students.

Nonetheless it's clear that in general one ought to avoid offending people if one seeks to maintain a mutually respectful and productive relationship with them. Furthermore, giving offense can be an indication that one has denigrated or denied full membership status to an individual. Such an offense may be based upon a reasonable judgment that the student's status or personhood has been denied. In one sense, it appears odd that we would consider questions related to justification of offense because people may have a hard time controlling whether they are offended. When students come to a campus to study, they bring with them values that they may not have analyzed critically and, like all people, they are offended by certain acts. This is not to say that being offended has no adequate basis. Generally some argument (even an inchoate one) lies behind the taking of offense. For example, a student who has taken offense from an angry professor might say, "The professor shouldn't yell at us like that for no reason." Such offense is predicated on an understanding that a basic norm of human conduct has been violated. One thought one had a legitimate expectation of certain behavior on the part of the other party, which is subsequently not observed. It appears then that we can distinguish justified offense, based upon reasonable expectations, from unjustified offense (based on unreasonable or false expectations).

Let us consider an example of student offense, with a view toward assessing its reasonability and the respectfulness of professorial treatment of students. A student may be offended that a professor assumes the legitimacy of an evolutionary approach in accounting for biological phenomena.

However, such offense cannot be sustained in secular institutions of higher education that have endorsed evolution as the ruling theoretical paradigm, particularly in the sciences. To be offended, however, by professorial subscription to a theoretical viewpoint endorsed by a secular institution of higher education reveals naiveté about the way secular higher education functions. In any case, students cannot legitimately expect that professors will not assert things with which students disagree, although this implies that students are wrong in some of their beliefs. Professors do have a right, however, to deny the validity of students' beliefs and may have reason to do so. For example, the professor who teaches using an evolutionary framework that will not allow any supernatural data will perforce not consider a student's explanation of creation ex nihilo as valid, and will deny the legitimacy of that explanation. The professor who believes that history is cyclical will undoubtedly point out to students who believe in the linearity of history that their views have significant problems that, the professor believes, cannot be addressed satisfactorily. The professor who has come to a settled belief that relativism as a philosophy is bankrupt will be inclined, if not obligated, to demonstrate to students who hold to relativism the insurmountable intellectual issues they must address, thereby telling them unmistakably that their beliefs won't pass the tests necessary to give them credence.

When professors do deny the validity of students' beliefs, they need to retain respect even within disagreement, questioning, gentle correction, and so on. Professors should avoid ridicule of students no matter how uninformed, unreasonable, or even uncivil their views seem to be. In ridiculing a position, such as creationism or Biblical literalism, a professor may claim (or even intend) to only denigrate the misinformed view and not the student. But this distinction tends to be irrelevant in practice. Regardless of the aim of the ridicule, the insulting tone of the professor's retort will tend to implicate the student whose view is being criticized. If the view is described as ignorant, it is a short inference to conclude that those who hold and assert the view are also being called ignorant. When a belief (or theory or activity) is central to the lives and self-understandings of students, its denigration by the professor becomes an insult to the student's intellectual and moral capacity and the significance of his or her life—an assault on the student's personhood.

Such insults not only may do damage to students' self-respect, but they may also cut off students from full participation in the classroom. A student whose view is ridiculed is unlikely to speak up again or devote his or her energies to succeeding in the course. By cutting off such a student's participation, the professor loses a chance for productive dialogue with the student and his or her view. Professors who deal harshly with opposing views may lose an opportunity to win serious consideration of the merits of their own views from such students. Furthermore, taking up and responding to objections in a civil manner has more value for the intellectual inquiry of the class than does dismissing challenges and skepticism out of hand. That is, biology teachers do well to explain why they adopt evolution by natural selection and how they think this approach answers objections from creationists and supporters of intelligent design. A respectful presentation of the merits of a theory vis-à-vis alternatives can help to demonstrate the reasoning and presuppositions of each view as well as the nature of current intellectual and social debate. (See Blanco, 2005; Bush, 2005; Collins, 2005; Friedlander, 2005; and Shapiro, 2005; for a discussion about this point in relation to intelligent design and evolution.)

This implies that in responding to views that the professor finds objectionable or ignorant, the professor should use reason rather than ridicule to maximize intellectual engagement and understanding in the course. To the extent that professors are critical of student views, they should attempt insofar as possible to distinguish between the problematic assertion by the student and the student himself or herself. For example, the professor should attempt to avoid displaying attitudes of anger, impatience, disgust, or dismay toward students when responding to their views. While objecting to the student's view, the professor should indicate acceptance of the student as an individual with potential for intelligent thought and moral agency, and treat the student as a welcome member of the course (for example, by showing willingness to continue to dialogue with the student in the future).

A recent example of professorial disrespect for students' religious views has received considerable press. University of Kansas Religious Studies Professor Paul Mirecki had planned to teach a course titled "Special Topics in Religion: Intelligent Design, Creationism, and other Religious Mythologies." He sent an email discussing his plans for the course "to members of a student organization [in which he] referred to religious conservatives as 'fundies' and said a course describing intelligent design as mythology would be a 'nice slap in their big fat face.'" Mirecki's email was circulated to the wider public and he was roundly rebuked, including by university Chancellor Robert Hemenway, who claimed that other emails written by Mirecki were "repugnant and vile" for their views toward Catholics and other Christians (The Associated Press, 2005). Mirecki apologized, withdrew the course he had proposed, and was forced to step down as department chair.

In this example, it appears that the professor had planned a course (at least in part) to shock and insult a group of people. With such an intention behind it, the conduct of the class itself would almost certainly display disrespect for the views of fundamentalist Christian students. Such students would be and would feel unwelcome and excluded from full participation. Of course, Mirecki's statement about the course and use of the denigrating term "fundies" was made outside of the classroom environment. Presumably he thought the content of his email would not be circulated to the general public. Yet respect owed students extends outside of the classroom and includes interaction with students in clubs, advising, and informal encounters. Mirecki probably assumed, perhaps with reason, that the members of the student club he was talking to shared his rejection of creationism and religious fundamentalism more generally. If professors know themselves to be talking out of earshot of students or talking to like-minded individuals, then disrespectful speech about a differing view would seem to be harmless. Nonetheless, one should be careful about assuming that all members of a group—even a group generally formed to advance a particular ideology (college Democrats, Republicans, Feminists, Rifle Club, Environmentalists, and so on)—share the same views. Some students in any setting may have sympathies for opposing views and still be insulted at the denigration. Regardless of its effect on those to whom the professor speaks, demeaning language is problematic. Public awareness of a disrespectful professorial attitude compromises a professor's ability to maintain student respect and provide a fair and accessible forum in the classroom. Therefore faculty are professionally responsible for avoiding demeaning statements which could possibly become public knowledge.

Animosity regarding opposing or differing political and religious views is common today. It would be difficult to fault Mirecki or anyone else for sometimes feeling and wanting to express his low opinion of perceived political opponents. Nonetheless, for the sake of effective and supportive teaching, professors are responsible for restraining their disrespect—particularly in public discourse. Publicly engaging in or even allowing such expressions to become public exacerbates polarization and detracts from the intellectual and social life of the campus and classroom.

Educators can disrespect students without even intending to attack them or their views. The professor may casually refer to his or her own views as true or commonly accepted, without acknowledging that some present in the class may hold different views. For example, a social science professor may contrast Eastern religions with what he or she calls "our religion," meaning Christianity. Such statements assume that all members of the class are Christian and, unwittingly, imply that non-Christian students are not fully part of the group. A professor need not keep his or her own religious or political beliefs silent, such as by hiding crosses, leaving one's yarmulke at home, or scrupulously avoiding any reference to attendance of religious services. However, professors should avoid casual assertion of their religious or political views as clearly true and good, such that these would be agreed to by all right-thinking persons. Such suggestions, even when made unwittingly, insult and exclude those who possess different views.

What constitutes disrespect, and thus justifies being called offense, in education depends in part upon the setting. For example, students who attend an institution of higher education affiliated with and committed by mission to further a particular religious viewpoint could expect a sympathetic treatment of this religion. If the school religion accepts the Genesis account of creation as the literal truth, students could expect that a biology instructor will not assume the truth of evolution. In such a context, one would expect that any discussion of Darwinian evolution would make note of this theory's conflict with the school's tradition and the students' views. Students could expect a discussion of religious approaches to biology either in this course or in alternative offerings. In the context of a religious school, students could expect professors to sometimes refer to the truth or goodness of the official religion as a clear presupposition.

Students of different faiths and beliefs who attended the school could not expect the religious neutrality required of a public institution. They should not be offended by assertions of religious community that are not intended to insult or exclude them.

Of course, regardless of the affiliation of the school, some basic respect for all persons is warranted. Neither public nor private religiously affiliated schools should explicitly demean particular religious views, Catholicism or Judaism, both because one ought not assault the personhood of members of that faith present in the class and because of a general duty to foster civic values in all students. Furthermore, regardless of the affiliation and orientation of a school, there is value in fair-minded consideration of alternatives, and discussion of these should be welcome.

Profanity and Obscenity in the Classroom

We have noted that the nature of a particular academic subject may evoke offense from students even when students cannot justify their unease based on good academic reasons. We want to press this point a bit because in some academic fields, particularly arts and letters, the very nature of the treatment of a subject may be intended to evoke controversy. In literature, for example, an author may use scatological language to identify the character of a fictive person. In the arts, nude figures in paintings and sculptures are not uncommon historically, and students studying drawing may be required to practice drawing using live nude models. The recent use of cadavers in artistic works has raised eyebrows and ethical questions (Lost Budgie Blog, 2005; Veith, 2005). In theater, students may be required to perform roles that include suggestive or titillating dialogue. Cinematic classes may require students to view films that contain plentiful profanity, nudity, and erotic encounters. Students, for various reasons, may find themselves offended by the types of art we have listed. What responsibility does a professor have to these students to treat them respectfully?

We see three possible responses a professor could make to students who are offended by various artistic expressions or their counterparts in other disciplines. First, the professor can say, essentially, "You don't belong here. Study something else." However this viewpoint may be expressed, it has the force of inferring that criticism of the academic discipline is out of the question, except on grounds that those within the discipline deem acceptable. Without exploring questions related to aesthetics and critical professional judgment, we merely assert that in the classroom, no viewpoint is above judicious criticism. To tell students that because of their perspectives they are not fit for a particular discipline is to close the door on certain sources of critical assessment of the discipline and is perforce contrary to the educational enterprise. A student may come to see an unbridgeable mismatch between his or her viewpoints and the viewpoints informing a particular discipline, but that perception should arise from the student (unless a lack of merit-based respect signals to a student that his or her abilities are not in sync with his or her academic aspirations). That a student does not appreciate or subscribe to the depiction of nudity in art does not mean the student should be demeaned. However, the student's views will most likely preclude serious critical engagement with art, including the student's ability to adequately explain why one could consider nudity a viable component of artistic expression. Thus, in all likelihood, the student's merit-based respect will suffer on purely academic grounds. In courses designed to introduce nonmajors to a topic, the need for explaining why particular expressions of artistic temperament are considered legitimate, though offensive to some, is even more important than such an apologia for devotees. Respect for students entails that their objections be answered professionally, not with disdain.

To respect students who object to particular treatment of artistic subjects does not entail that students' responses are automatically considered valuable. Some student statements are not very good contributions to a discussion. In these cases, the professor should still respond respectfully, possibly trying to find a kernel of insight in the student's statement or gently reasserting the main thread of discussion. The professor has a responsibility to keep these students as welcome members of the class who potentially can comprehend the material being presented and ultimately can make good contributions to the class.

The second response a professor could make to students who are offended by various artistic expressions would be acknowledgment and explanation. We have already hinted at this response above. In effect, the professor acknowledges that people can take offense at a particular work of art, and may even go on to show examples of such offense in what many might consider inoffensive art today. For example, is Michelangelo's David offensive? If so, why? What constitutes legitimate offense? In other words, the recognition of offense becomes an opportunity to help students work through concepts related to what constitutes legitimate offense in regard to artistic works. This approach has the virtue of seizing the moment by antic-ipating potential offense and using it to explain to students the issues relat-ed to artistic intent and the reasons why particular artists have used provocative artworks.

The third response a professor could make to students who are offended by various artistic expressions would be accommodation. It may be the case that students can be given choices about which poems, nov-els, plays, and artifacts in the fine arts they want to study. To the extent that such choices are viable given the course under consideration, choice is an appropriate way to handle student qualms about offensive works. In reality, however, courses that include what some might consider offensive materials generally do so because the course requires some familiarity with those materials. An art education that excluded all nude forms or a literature education that excluded all profane language would be grossly incomplete by the standards of most any expert.

As we argued in Chapter 1, academic freedom includes the provision that professors, as experts, have the freedom to make choices about course content within the purview of legitimate expectations about what content a course offers. What we have not discussed thus far are professorial speech, acts, and comportment that could be considered offensive. For example, does academic freedom protect professorial use of vulgar, profane, or inflammatory speech? Even in dress and personal presentation, are there limits on the forms of expression that are appropriate for faculty?

As we asserted in Chapter 1, ethical standards can be invoked to establish principles sharing widespread or universal acceptance. However, when dealing with ethical issues related to speech, gestures, and dress, we think it important to address the issue of cultural change—particularly because one argument against a discussion of the ethical issues could assert that changing cultural standards make moot such a discussion. That is, cultural relativism could be used to claim that values are defined by local customs enshrined in contemporary conduct. No universal principles of conduct regarding speech, gestures, and dress are possible, so local, contemporary values are the sole criteria for judging suitability in the three areas of professorial conduct cited. Ultimately we reject this line of argument, but initially we will engage it to show its weaknesses.

We acknowledge that cultural standards change, even within a particular culture or subculture. The present fashion of women publicly exposing their midriffs is a distinct change from, say, apparel norms in the 1950s. Tattoos, once identified with men in the military services and members of motorcycle gangs, are now au courant. Bra burning by women in the 1960s signaled not only a comment about what constitutes appropriate undergarments but also what constitutes oppressive undergarments. Changes in clothing styles, therefore, often signal changes in cultural norms—or at least challenges to cultural norms. The change from a U.S. culture that tended toward formality in the 1950s (men wore ties and suits to church) to a culture now that prizes individuality and informality (men can wear jeans to church while drinking Starbucks coffee) tells us that clothing fashion is not isolated from the values a culture promotes. The same can be said of language and gestures. Even a passing review of American movies made during the last 50 years shows that restrictions on scatological language, nudity, and horrific images have decreased. Cultural standards, including dress and language habits, do not have to be taken for granted and can be subjected to rational criticism.

Indeed, cultural change is fueled by changes in ideas about what constitutes right and wrong conduct. Cultural relativism cannot properly undercut moral discussion by appealing to societal acceptance of change as good—or bad. In fact, the values that support change are at issue, and even if a correction is needed to bring particular cultural practices in line with ethical values based on a universal standard, that correction has to be critiqued morally as to whether it did in fact make a proper adjustment. By raising the issue of cultural relativism, we intend to show (1) that we cannot appeal to the way a culture operates as hermetically sealed so that no appeal to principles beyond those allowed by the dominant culture are permissible and (2) that moral discussion must be informed by principles, such as respect of personhood, that are universal.

The recommendation of universal standards, especially with regard to language and dress, is unpopular today. Commentators on culture and the university from across the political spectrum have tended to argue against stipulating moral aims and guidelines for the university. Both "left-wing" postmodernists and "right-wing" libertarians demonstrate skepticism about any common moral standards. Other conservatives today suspect any attempt by universities and faculty to formulate and advocate a moral agenda as liberal brainwashing. In this climate, argues O'Brien (1998):

> When push cometh to shove, one can be reasonably cer-
> tain that the freedom to "choose" a life style and stance
> will overcome any qualms about moral worth of the
> claim. In an academic arena—particularly the modern
> university—the claim for free assertion is a virtual
> absolute . . . [which] undercuts moral discussion. (pp.
> 69–70)

Nonetheless, we hold that it is necessary to recognize limits on con-duct even in the areas in which culture and individuals gravitate toward increasing latitude in choice. Despite tremendous actual and justifiable difference in norms of dress and speech, we believe some principles regarding conduct can be identified that hold across culture and situa-tion. These include respect for personhood and the maintenance of dig-nified, mutually fulfilling, and productive relationships between individuals. Ultimately the debate is not about whether persons should be respected, as we have already shown, but how that respect should be manifested.

Because ideas inform cultural standards of dress, speech, and gestures, professors should consider the import of those ideas regarding their own dress, speech, and gestures. Again we emphasize that students can take offense for indefensible reasons, so it is virtually impossible to determine a priori how any individual student will respond to professorial dress, speech, or gestures. For example, a student could take offense when a professor wears a tie to class every day, believing that the professor is making a state-ment about being superior by "dressing up" (Sperber, 2005, p. B20; for a counterexample see Lang, 2005). Whether that is the professor's intention is immaterial because the student infers that such is the case by the mere presence of a tie. Some students might find a professor's use of scatological language amusing and take no offense, but student acceptance (or rejection) of a particular professorial habit is not an infallible guide to determining whether professorial speaking, gestures, or dress are either inoffensive or offensive; Benton (2004a) makes this very point.

Concerning dress, as professionals, professors can mistakenly take the position that what they wear is their own business and should not be prescribed. First, such a position does not take into account one's professional duties as a professor. A professor has an obligation to comport himself or herself in a manner conducive to education. To the extent that clothing can become a distraction to the classroom process of education, professors should use professional judgment in the attire they wear. We can offer no hard-and-fast rule about what to wear because institutional expectations, geographical locale, professional considerations, and personal preference all play some role in making decisions about professional classroom attire. We are aware of one U.S. college that maintains the long-standing tradition of professors wearing their academic regalia to class. Inappropriate? Not for the norm of that institution. But for students at most institutions, that practice—although harkening to the Middle Ages and thus having a long pedigree—would appear odd, perhaps offensive. Printed debate about professorial clothing provides a great deal of advice—at times contradictory—that is worth considering (Benton, 2004a, 2004b; Evans, 2004; Johnson, 1998; Lang, 2005; Malloy, 1998; Nicholson, 1998; Perlmutter, 2004; Sawyer, 1998; Schneider, 1998; Waks, 1998; Wilhite, 1998).

Aside from issues of distraction from education, there are moral reasons to object to clothing which reveals more of the body than customary in professional settings. Perlmutter (2004) frankly acknowledges the problem of scantily clothed students and, by extension, scantily clothed professors. In a sense it seems odd to say that dress involves an assault on or disrespect to the personhood of others (as long as no denigrating epithets are printed on the clothing). The scantily clad student or professor does not necessarily make any statement about any other individual, and would not seem to do any mental, much less physical, damage to the normally constituted observer. Nonetheless, when an individual fails to follow the norms of a professional setting, this displays a lack of seriousness in the endeavor and a lack of concern for the reception of the audience. The point is not that revealing a certain part of the body is absolutely immoral. Rather, by mutual understanding individuals agree to cover the body in certain ways in professional settings—those who neglect to do so violate the mutual understanding symbolic of civil interaction.

To limit choices of clothing to personal preference is to ignore the fact that people judge each other—probably in larger part than they are willing to admit (Perlmutter, 2004)—based on looks, including clothing. In fact, the type of clothes a person wears signals particular values. To dress informally can signal approachableness, but informal dress can also signal lack of standards. Although linking values with informal dress may be criticized as endorsing stereotypes, the fact remains that clothing signals values, a point Sperber (2005) makes by showing that the teaching values he ascribed to teachers who dressed formally were incorrect. He revised his stereotypical notions—his prejudices about the relationship between certain styles of clothing and their relationship to effective teaching—discovering that "I wasn't as laid back as my appearance implied" (p. B20). In fact, because fashions do change, Sperber counsels that "in a long teaching career, every instructor should have three- to five-year checkups and revise their dress, approach, and material as their personal values and circumstances change" (p. B20). That appears to us as good advice, but we add two caveats. First, legitimate offense to personhood based on maintaining dignity in the human community should also be a consideration in determining clothing choices for the classroom. Second, the match between teaching style and dress cannot trump ethical conduct. Although consistency between dress and teaching philosophy can be a valuable pedagogical tool in helping students match expectations with demeanor, nothing requires professors to wear a suit if they categorize their teaching style as quite formal. However, the requirement for ethical conduct (even when the match between clothing and teaching style is a nice fit) stands, regardless of the external portrayal of an inward attitude. Indeed, when clothing and teaching do fit but conspire against ethical conduct, the point of the fit is absolutely vitiated.

Profanity

Concerning speech and gestures, does academic freedom guarantee that a professor can use "dirty" language and profane gestures? Academic freedom does not say that professors can choose to do whatever they like to do or that if they believe something is appropriate it cannot be challenged legitimately. Let's say that a professor punctuated his or her lectures with vulgar language. Could such a practice be justified under any circumstance? The types of questions we would need to ask could help us make some determination about justification in this case. Was the language in keeping with the topic of the lecture? If the professor was lecturing about communication habits among particular groups of professionals—including organized gang leaders, clergy, Fortune 500 executives, and professors—and presenting research that showed certain language patterns (in this case vulgar language) are common to all groups, the professor might use vulgar language to describe typical uses. But is that the best way to make the pedagogical point? This question is not entirely transparent because what constitutes the "best" way is, to some extent, dependent on the particular context and judgment of the professor. However, we can ask whether other ways would be as effective and entail less risk in terms of offending students. Surely when a professor does punctuate a lecture with vulgar language, the potential for offense is quite high and the question of whether the pedagogical intent will be lost, given the offense, is not an insignificant concern. "Object lessons" of the sort we have cited are risky, and cost-benefit analyses generally tend to counsel caution in using them.

But what if a professor is quoting the use of scatological language? For example, a historian describing a conflict between two figures might describe one as telling the other to "fuck off." Or a professor of literature might read a poem in class that uses what are considered taboo words. We cannot dismiss the possibility that such occurrences can be legitimate. However, we also cannot dismiss the powerful feelings and images such words convey and the highly likely possibility that some in the class will consider them offensive precisely because the words are generally used to convey disrespect. To what extent and in what way profane language involves disrespect depends upon context and the type of locution.

Professors who just mention profane words (say, in a list of taboo words) do not really use the word, and thus do not invoke its complete meaning and suggestiveness of disrespect for personhood. A professor who uses the word in a description of an imagined dialogue or to swear at a third party not present (the U.S. government, Al Qaeda, a criminal) does use the word, but does not direct it at the student. A professor swearing at a student conveys disrespect for the individual's value, and thus this use should always be avoided. Other uses of profanity, because they evoke a situation of disrespect between persons, may also have costs. Professors who use them regularly, particularly if they appear angry or otherwise out of control, convey disrespect for humanity. The professor is also likely to lose the respect of students and have a more difficult time functioning as a leader and authority in the class, detracting from the quality of education provided.

Again, the professor needs to ensure that the use of speech and symbols generally considered offensive be grounded in solid pedagogical justification. We reject two common justifications that faculty might give for regular use of profanity: "That's how I am" and the "real world" justifications. The "That's how I am" justification assumes that the way a person behaves is just part and parcel of the person and is beyond question. Sometimes this justification is used to mitigate offense as when a person says, "Don't take offense at what he said. He talks like that to everyone." That a person is rude, ill-mannered, vulgar, bitingly sarcastic, or in some other way offensive equally to all is not an adequate recommendation to accept the person's behavior. Consistently offensive behavior is simply consistently offensive, not justified. Indeed the "That's how I am" argument really is evidence that a person's behavior needs to be altered so that offense is gradually minimized with the hope of being eradicated.

The "real world" argument is also used at times to defend bad pedagogical practices that create offense. In undergraduate professional programs, a professor in social work or psychology might try to justify offensive speech or gestures by saying that students need to know what happens in the kind of environment in which they will work. Showing films with sexual encounters and using explicit language to describe those encounters, according to the "real world" argument, is perfectly justifiable. However, it is one thing to alert students to the social conditions in which they will work by explaining to them what those encounters most likely will be like—it is yet another thing to show the graphic details of sexual encounters. A professor may seek to depict typical sexual behavior to increase student familiarity. On the other hand, it's not clear what advantage exists in witnessing sexuality in action as opposed to reading about it. Shocking students who are sensitive to depictions of sex in general or offended by particular practices that they oppose, such as homosexuality, doesn't constitute a pedagogical justification. Professors would have to make a case that depicting various sexual practices makes these practices understandable to students in a way that cannot be described in literature.

The greatest basis for student discomfort would be depictions of abusive or otherwise unhealthy sexual practices, such as bestiality or self-mutilation. On one hand, it seems that professors should hope and expect that students will not be privy to these sorts of encounters, such that rehearsing them for students would be of little use to them. On the other hand, students might work with clients who have been subjected to such treatment or have perpetrated it themselves. Take, for example, the pedagogical problem in a social work class of how to impress upon students the trauma associated with rape victims and how social workers address such trauma. Clearly the professor of such a class could provide films that explain what constitutes rape, contain interviews of people who have been raped, show pictures of the physical results of rape (including graphic images of traumatized genitalia), and so forth. But is there a need to show an actual rape? If there is a justified pedagogical need, shouldn't the rape be shown with the utmost caution so that no appearance of salaciousness is being evoked in the audience? Sensitivity to the personhood of students is a critical factor in making pedagogical decisions that have a high potential to evoke offense.

Again, the pedagogical intent is paramount, and pedagogical justification can include sensitizing students to situations that they may consider abnormal so that they can effectively help clients in those situations. To genuinely help those who are engaged in destructive behaviors does not entail either that the student as helper-in-training engage in those behaviors or condone them. It does entail that students gain a degree of sympathy for the plight of those engaged in destructive behaviors so that students, when they become professional helpers, treat their clients with respect. It is not clear that by submitting students to the graphic details of such behaviors engenders respect for clients.

Reasons and Remedies for Disrespect

Presumably, most professors do not set out to disrespect their students. Having evinced disrespect for their students, many professors offer apologies and feel regret for their conduct. Despite these good intentions, evidence suggests (Bain, 2004) that certain patterns of disrespect are endemic in the academy. If faculty and institutions are to prevent such conduct and its effects, they would benefit from an analysis of the causes of disrespect. We see at least five explanations for failures of respect in higher education.

One problem that causes disrespect is professorial dogmatism. Academics come to view themselves as experts whose theories and approaches to their subject matter are beyond dispute. From such certitude the professor may conclude that any who disagree are misguided and ignorant. This may have been the problem in the Mirecki case, as Mirecki was so certain of his own belief in Darwinian evolution that he despised those who defended an alternative view. Getting beyond such disrespect requires either that professors acknowledge that other views might have value or, minimally, that proponents of such views deserve personhood and role respect no matter how lacking in merit the professor believes their views to be.

In addition to dogmatic defense of a view, disrespect is fueled by polarization and a combat mentality. Many academics have long perceived themselves as fighting for causes in their teaching and research. Academics find themselves involved in culture wars, predominantly the struggle between "left" and "right," but also other struggles over disciplinary approaches and theories. This sense of polarization has intensified since 9/11 and the Bush administration's subsequent war on terror and Iraq War. Because of a sense of increased political stakes, professors may feel called on to act decisively. Furthermore, faculty may perceive themselves to be under attack: For example, liberal faculty by new calls for censorship and surveillance, and conservative faculty by the relative

predominance of liberal views and criticism of the Republican administration on campuses. In addition to engagement in the struggle over
ideas, faculty sometimes experience personal attacks as students or colleagues malign their ideologies, religions, or sexual identities.

Academics' understanding of themselves as involved in combat makes
those with opposing views, including one's students, into an enemy. In this
climate of polarization, faculty may disrespect students in anger. Or they
may demean class members with opposing views in order to help secure
their own side's victory in the classroom. Indeed, one might speculate that
such political polarization, and its concomitant resentment and strategiz-
ing, led to Mirecki's denigration of conservative Christians. In a recent
commentary on the politics of teaching today, Willis (2005) describes her
own sense of being under siege as an academic:

> For the right, "liberal" has become an epithet—roughly
> equivalent to the "Godless Communist" of an earlier
> era—that applies to anyone who is not a conservative
> Republican or a Christian fundamentalist. Most people
> who are attracted to academic life fit that definition for
> fairly obvious reasons: We prefer reading, writing and
> research to business; care more about job security than
> the chance to get rich; and are comfortable with (secular)
> Enlightenment values. (p. B11)

A wag has quipped that there are two types of people: those who
divide everything into two types and those who don't. The problem of
dividing things into either one of two types is that no shades of gray
remain and the polarization intensifies the conflict. Willis may be right
about conservative exaggeration in attacks on liberals. Yet she herself slips
into a blanket suggestion that conservatives are out of place in academia,
and thus perpetuates political polarization while she protests against it.
Denying that conservatives have sincere interests in inquiry cuts off the
possibility of dialogue with them. To the extent that educators carry this
attitude into their classes, equal opportunity for all students is undermined.
Even if professors have themselves been treated disrespectfully, they have
an obligation to continue to show respect for students and colleagues.

This is true, in part, because even the most disrespectful student deserves some respect by a faculty member for his or her potential as an intellectual and moral agent, a feeling person who should not be abused, and a paying student who has a right to inclusion in the course. Furthermore, if the faculty member breaches norms of respect for students, this is likely to undermine the sense of control and comfort conducive to classroom learning. For this reason, professors do well to try to overcome the sense of being in the trenches in the classroom. If the professor disarms, students may follow.

The instructor who implies that everyone believes or should believe like himself or herself may do so out of arrogance or polarizing defensiveness, but need not. Disrespect is sometimes caused by a third factor, the misunderstanding or lack of awareness of diverse views. Ignorance of other perspectives can lead one to treat insensitively those who hold them, causing insult and exclusion. Faculty fresh out of graduate school may not be aware of the extent to which many students may not share their secular intellectual approaches. Lack of knowledge and awareness of student religious beliefs may lead faculty to be less than sensitive in responding to student skepticism about empirical science and its conclusions. Greater faculty education in student beliefs and how to address them respectfully would assist with this problem.

A fourth possible reason for professorial disrespect for students is a mismatch of expectations between professors and students. Boyer (1987) captures this mismatch in his research on the undergraduate experience in America:

> At a freshman psychology lecture we attended, 300 students were still finding seats when the professor started talking. "Today," he said into the microphone, "we will continue our discussion of learning." He might as well have been addressing a crowd in a Greyhound bus terminal. Like commuters marking time until their next departure, students in this class alternately read the newspaper, flipped through a paperback novel, or propped their feet on the chairs ahead of them, staring into space. Only when the professor defined a term

which, he said, "might appear on an exam" did they look up and start taking notes.

What we found in many classrooms was a mismatch between faculty and student expectations, a gap that left both parties unfulfilled. Faculty, concerned with scholarship, wanted to share ideas with students, who were expected to appreciate what professors do. . . .

As for students, they are remarkably conscious of grades, willing to conform to the formula for success. A sophomore in a pre-med program said she wanted her courses to be spelled out "with no surprises. My goal is to get a good background so I can pass the MCAT [Medical College Admission Test] and I'm not interested in hearing about the professor's Ph.D. dissertation."

"A college degree isn't enough," said one honors student. "You've got to have a good GPA to get into graduate school, or get a first-rate job." Another commented: "People at this college are very resume-conscious. Undergraduates are afraid of controversy. They hesitate to participate in vigorous give and take on any topic. The main thing is to prepare for the exam." (pp. 140–141)

The mismatch Boyer highlights is common and can be the cause of frustration—and disrespect—on both sides of the lecture. Faculty expect students to share their love of their discipline, intellectual issues, and the learning process. Professors take their teaching seriously because they believe that what they have to offer students is important. Such an attitude is entirely appropriate, else why teach? Why work with students to help them learn if what one teaches is of little moment? When students show no interest in learning, besides what is required to get an acceptable grade, professors can lose their respect for students. Yet students still deserve respect as persons and class members.

Overcoming the disrespect of the disappointed professor requires, in part, realigning expectations. Professors should not act continually surprised at students' limitations. Nor should they expect all or most students to be above average. Faculty teaching at any but elite schools must recognize that most of their students will lack their instructors' interests and abilities. Some moderation in expectation can increase faculty satisfaction with student performance and toleration of error.

Student disinterest may also mean that faculty need to alter course content. Faculty should attempt to take into account student interests and abilities in constructing courses, rather than planning courses for ideal young academics. This does not mean that professors should defer absolutely to student preferences. There are frequently ways to make material more interesting and accessible without throwing out or "dumbing down" the curriculum. Professors should teach in the way likely to lead to the most learning of the subject matter for that group of students. This may mean incorporating attention-getting devices (such as multimedia presentations) and active learning (to get students involved who respond to hands-on work).

Professors disgusted with student disengagement should consider whether their courses can be reconceptualized to encourage positive student involvement. This can renew the professors' respect for students and level of engagement with the class. We believe that professors have the creativity to investigate sources of disrespect and do whatever is needed to change their disrespect into respect for students. A variety of sources on effective teaching provide all kinds of pedagogical methods that can aid professors in reconceptualizing their approach to teaching so that disrespect is eliminated (Andrews, Garrison, & Magnusson, 1996; Baiocco & DeWaters, 1998; Bess, 1982; Brookfield, 1991; Brown & Atkins, 1988; Chickering & Gamson, 1987; Eble, 1990; Ericksen, 1984; Feldman, 1988; Findley, 1995; Menges, Weimer, & Associates, 1996; Roth, 1997; Svinicki & Menges, 1996).

The first place to start is probably by differentiating between merit-based respect and students' personhood and status as students. Just because students don't have a professor's devotion to a particular discipline does not mean that students should be treated disrespectfully. Professors really do have a major role in doing their best to ensure that their disciplinary approaches appeal to students instead of assuming that students should like to study what interests professors.

A fifth cause of disrespectful teaching is professorial fatigue in facing the same challenges with the same limited results year in and year out.

Faculty burnout can be the cause for some despair leading to disrespect. After answering the same ill-informed question or perspective the umpteenth time, a professor could respond with disrespect for students, writing demeaning comments on students' papers, and giving students a look that says, "Now that really was a stupid question." The solution to this cause of disrespect—get revitalized—can be difficult to enact, especially if a professor has become jaded. Going to conferences that address how to teach the Millennials, reading intensely in pedagogy, applying for a sabbatical, seeking a nonteaching assignment for a semester, applying for a professorial exchange program, securing employment at a different institution, taking a leave of absence, even retiring are ways to address the burnout that causes disrespect for students. Ultimately, however, professors need to cope with the fact that teaching is a service that attends to all-too-common errors in the learning enterprise. To enable students to recognize errors of all sorts, correct them, and construct solid intellectual credentials is an ongoing task that may not receive rewards the professor believes are commensurate with the sometimes grinding effort required to ply the teaching trade. Other than professional accomplishment, is there ever any reward—economic or otherwise—that can compensate for endless hours grading research papers?

When professors lose respect for students, they have little reason to make efforts to aid them. Investments in the student's education may appear to be (at best) wasted time or (at worst) aiding and abetting of a dangerous mind. We appeal to a service ethic in recommending an antidote to disrespect. If students do not respond appropriately to professorial service, one of two reasons may explain their inappropriate responses. Either the students genuinely don't care about being educated, or the way they are being educated is less than satisfactory to them. We tend to believe that with few exceptions students do genuinely care about learning and respond positively when they are engaged to learn effectively. This does not mean that students automatically respond positively to every useful effort to help them learn. However, when they are offered diverse types of presentation and assessment, asked to produce a significant amount of high-level work, and challenged in various other ways, students generally come to see the value and the pleasure of learning. The presupposition that students really do like to learn means that the onus for engaging students in the learning process starts with the professor. As with the overly high expectations that are its frequent precursor, fatigue does not justify professors losing their concern for their students as persons and potential learners.

Conclusion

In conclusion, our discussion of respectful treatment of students implies the following norms of professorial conduct:

1) Professors should generally treat students with respect by:
   - Acknowledging and rewarding student academic merit and achievements
   - Providing educational opportunity, inclusion in course participation, and concern for the progress and well-being of all students assigned to the professor's tutelage and care
   - Recognizing and refraining from assaulting the student as a human being, a rational person, and a moral agent

2) Regarding language and manner in their teaching and public discourse, professors should generally:
   - Refrain from directly, or by implication, demeaning the intelligence or moral worth of groups of people
   - Discuss ideas and identities in a way that acknowledges and welcomes differing views, including all as members in the classroom

3) With respect to unconventional dress, profane language, and graphic materials, professors should avoid material and practices which:
   - Connote disrespect for persons and the educational process
   - Lack sufficient pedagogical value to justify their use

4) Professors (individually) and institutions (collectively) should work to curb attitudes that lead to disrespectful treatment of students. In particular, faculty should attempt to curb the tendencies of:
   - Dogmatic dismissal of opposing views
   - Angry or strategic polarization of disagreements
   - Ignorance about and insensitivity toward diverse views
   - Disappointment due to unrealistic expectations
   - Fatigue with the teaching process and its results

6

Faculty-Student Relationships

The educational importance of the faculty-student relationship is already evident in the foregoing chapters. As we said in Chapter 1, professors have a general duty to promote students' education and well-being. In Chapter 5, we argue that faculty should treat students with respect, avoiding denigration and disparagement. The analysis of the nature of a good faculty-student relationship also includes issues about boundaries. We begin by inquiring into the reasons and extent to which faculty ought to refrain from romantic relationships with students. We then discuss to what extent faculty should aim to or refrain from becoming friends with students. This discussion will lead to our own statement of the ideal form and goals of the faculty-student relationship.

Faculty-Student Romance

It is widely accepted today that faculty should not become romantically involved with their students. (Except when noted, we will use the terms "romantic" and "sexual" interchangeably throughout this discussion.) The prohibition of sexual involvement with students has been incorporated into university faculty codes of conduct. Indeed, if one were to ask anyone what the limits on faculty conduct with respect to their students are, one would expect sex to figure prominently—if not exclusively—in many responses. In our view, this reflects not just a general preoccupation with sex but also a sensitivity to its role in education.

Yet the rejection of faculty-student romance is fairly recent. By report, sexual relationships between faculty and students (especially male faculty and female students) have been common in academia. By some accounts, sleeping with one's professors has been a rite of passage for some female graduate students (Kipnis, 2004). Nor must one rely only on rumors and memoirs of secret encounters to find evidence of faculty-student romance. It is common to find married couples on campuses today who met when the female was a student in her future husband's class.

The tide turned against these relationships in the 1980s, influenced in no small part by the infusion of feminist consciousness into the academy. Billy Wright Dziech and Linda Weiner (1984) published *The Lecherous Professor*, exposing the extent of faculty sex with their students and condemning it as a form of sexual harassment. Subsequent treatment by ethicists such as Davis (1990), Tong (1999), and Superson (2001) have lent philosophical support to this condemnation. Courts have agreed that sexual harassment is involved, sometimes finding universities responsible for allowing sexual relations between faculty and students. Concern over litigation combined with ethics has resulted in a new institutional and individual consensus against faculty-student romance.

While it is widely agreed that such relationships are a problem, it is not as clear in the literature (much less individual and institutional opinions) what makes such relationships wrong, and thus exactly what the scope of policy should be in this regard. Dziech and Weiner's use of the term "lecher," although effective in swaying audiences to the generally good cause of greater vigilance regarding faculty relationships with students, is unfortunate insofar as it appeals to a vague and unreflective moralistic unease with sexual interests more generally. Lechery is not a sufficiently clear moral or legal term on which to base ethical judgment or school policy. What, then, is wrong with faculty sleeping with or otherwise becoming romantically involved with their students?

A salient feature of most imagined faculty-student relationships is age differences, with the relative youth of the student and seniority of the professor. In judging faculty-student relationships in primary and secondary education, age is the decisive factor. As children, precollege students are not able to freely consent to sexual encounters; adult seduction of such students amounts to statutory rape. Sexual activity is likely to be psychologically and physically harmful to a minor, adding to the offense and making the teacher's advance a violation of his or her basic duty to care for the student.

However, concerns about consent and sexual maturity are not decisive at the college level, where almost all students are at the age of legal consent. Most students have been sexually active by the time that they attend the university and almost all by the time they leave. Society still views as somehow unethical relationships between individuals significantly different in age, seemingly preferring heterosexual encounters of pairs who are the same age, the male perhaps slightly senior. However, we know of no research showing that other forms of relationship are unhealthy. Indeed, there is a long history of relationships between a mature senior partner and a younger member, many of which are viewed as successful and positive for both parties.

Furthermore, students are not necessarily much younger than faculty. Graduate students are generally close to the age of younger faculty members. With nontraditional students returning to college in droves, professors frequently face students their age or their seniors in undergraduate courses as well. Even if one were to reject any sexual relationship, in which, say, one party was more than one and a half times the age of the other (a principle that we do not defend), this would fail to rule out much faculty-student romance.

Faculty-student relationships are probably also thought to be inappropriate because of connotations of adultery. The classic case involves a married male professor who dallies with a student while never intending to leave his wife. Adultery is unethical insofar as the married individual breaks a promise to and deceives his spouse. If the adulterer also makes a false promise to his lover, then the affair involves deception of two parties. Insofar as adultery threatens marriages that are worth preserving, there is more reason that it should be avoided.

However, it must be recognized that not all faculty (or, of course, students) are married and that therefore faculty-student relationships need not involve adultery. Even married faculty may have an understanding with their spouses that they may have outside sexual relationships, such that no broken promises, deceit, or threats to the marriage are involved. Furthermore, although adultery is ethically problematic, it is legal in most of the United States—and neither government nor most private educational institutions enforce norms against it. Thus, although adultery is an additional ethical problem in much faculty-student romance, it is neither a universal feature of such relationships nor a sufficient basis for policies forbidding them. We need to examine what is wrong with faculty-student romance as such.

We have already alluded to the fact that such relationships occur disproportionately between male faculty and female students. Dziech and Weiner (1984) and subsequent commentators have argued that this shows the sexism of such relationships. Female students are singled out for faculty sexual attention. When women are treated differently from men in an institutional setting, this raises concerns of discrimination. Students should not be presented with additional burdens—or benefits—in the educational process because of their gender. Yet as Holmes (1996) notes, to say that such relationships are wrong because they discriminate is to beg the question. To be discriminatory, a form of treatment must not only be disproportional but also harm or disadvantage the group which is subject to it. If faculty romance with students is harmful for other reasons, then the fact that female students are disproportionate objects of such attention is evidence of a sexist system that disadvantages women.

Furthermore, if the fundamental problem of faculty-student relationships was discrimination, then only sexual relationships between male faculty and female students are wrong. However, most individuals and policies oppose all such relations, including those between female faculty and male students and faculty and students of the same gender. It could be argued that all of these are cases of sex discrimination insofar as the faculty member chooses a student based upon his or her own sexual preference. However, as some have noted, a bisexual professor could sleep with students of both genders, thus avoiding any charge of discrimination. Furthermore, although any student may be selected for faculty attention in part because of his or her gender, students are normally propositioned by professors for individual characteristics and not as mere representatives of a group. Again, to show the wrongness of such sexual attention by the faculty member, it must be demonstrated that it does a harm or other injustice to particular individuals—either the student who receives the faculty member's sexual attentions or the students who do not.

The Problem of Consent in Faculty-Student Relations

What is wrong with romantic relationships between faculty and students? The most obvious argument is that such relationships are not fully *consensual* and thus constitute coerced sex, and are thereby a form of harassment or rape. In the most obvious case, a professor might use his or her institutional power to *threaten* the student—either with a poor grade, a bad evaluation, or a negative vote on a thesis or other project. Because the victim exchanges sex for a passing grade, this has been called *quid pro quo* ("this for that") harassment. Such threats are clearly a form of coercion and invalidate any consent that the student gives. Although (as with sexual assault at gunpoint) the victim willingly agrees to engage in sexual acts under the conditions offered, the forced imposition of a limited choice makes the victim's participation coerced rather than voluntary. Academic goods such as grades, evaluations, and thesis completion are sufficiently important to a student's future success and well-being that she or he submits to a professor's sexual attention as a lesser, though still unwanted, evil. Because individuals should not suffer coercion, especially in matters central to their identity such as sexuality, such threats are clearly wrong and violations of basic respect for personhood.

A somewhat more complex situation is that of quid pro quo *offers*. In the offer, the professor suggests the exchange of a good grade or other evaluation for sexual favors from the student. As commentators such as Dixon (1996) note, the offer is not as clearly harmful to the student as the threat. In a sense, the student should be better off by having this option: If the student turns down the offer, by hypothesis, he or she could take the evaluation that he or she would have otherwise received. Thus the student is no worse off and, if she or he considers the good grade worth the sexual favor, is actually made better off.

Of course, a student might misjudge his or her own best interest in choosing to accept a sexual offer in exchange for a grade. For example, a student might fail to take into account risks of heartbreak, disease, pregnancy, or embarrassment. Given the flawed nature in human calculation and judgment, offers can sometimes make individuals worse off. However, the possibility of student miscalculation cannot be what makes offers wrong. We do not normally subject sexual offers to the test that they must improve an individual's well-being; few sexual propositions would be permissible on this score. We generally give individuals considerable leeway to enter relation-ships at their own risk. If we are to rule out offers by professors in partic-ular, we must argue that there is something particularly dangerous about such offers such that they constitute coercion or are very likely to harm the student, such that faculty wrong students by suggesting the trade.

However, there is reason to think that offers also pose a danger to stu-dents and are coercive. A student who is offered a good grade for sex with the professor may well understand an implied threat: Refusal may be punished with a bad grade. The professor has already indicated a will-ingness to give a grade that the student has not earned; he or she may be willing to give an undeservedly low grade as well as a high one. An indi-vidual who is using institutional power to secure sexual relations may become angry at being rebuffed and punish the student who rejects him. Thus sexual offers can also be treated as coercive harassment, even if they are not explicitly posed as such.

In addition to sexual coercion, quid pro quo threats and offers are also wrong for a different reason. Grades should be based on academic performance. To give them on any other basis corrupts education and violates the professor's responsibility to his or her institution, profession, and society. Giving inflated grades to students who sleep with the pro-fessor is unfair, as other students who had better academic performance receive equal or lower grades. It gives some students an opportunity for academic advancement unavailable to the rest, thus violating the princi-ple of equal treatment. Sex-for-grades trades probably also ultimately educationally disadvantage any students who accept them, insofar as the student has been allowed and encouraged to succeed without learning and studying academic material.

In summary, quid pro quo offers are wrong both because they lead to nonconsensual sex and because they corrupt and make unfair the acade-mic process. Professors who make such offers directly and explicitly mis-use their positions for self-interest. The professor shows maliciousness or thoughtlessness in seeking to gain power over the student and exhibits lack of professionalism in misusing education.

If use of the gradebook to force or encourage student sexual involve-ment with the professor is clearly wrong, what of relationships in which such threats and offers are not made? A professor might proposition a student and secure consent to sex without suggesting any repercussions or reward. Such seemingly voluntary relationships are harder to assimilate into the harassment or assault paradigm, because for behavior to constitute harassment or assault it must be *unwanted* by the victim.

However, it could be argued that student consent cannot ever be truly voluntary. Even if the professor makes no reference to the student's grades or academic progress, a student may have reason to believe that a threat is implicit in any sexual proposition. As Superson (2001) argues, evidence suggests that those with authority tend to retaliate against any rejection by their subordinates. If students reasonably fear retaliation, then it is questionable whether their consent is voluntary, regardless of any explicit threat. Dixon (1996) notes that this is supported by the "four large men argument": If four large individuals confronted a person in an alley and asked for 50 dollars, it is questionable whether money is freely given. For this reason, requests should not be made in the context of extreme power advantages, regardless of whether a threat is intended.

The logic of such an argument seems to have the counterintuitive implication that there can be no valid sexual propositions in contexts of power differentials. Such relationships occur all the time between rich and poor, socially connected and socially alienated, physically strong and weak, and supervisor and employee. Although the weaker party has some reason to fear offending the stronger, and has a considerable amount to gain from entering the relationship, neither law nor ethical judgment normally considers consent invalid in such contexts.

In response to this, we point out that the power of the gradebook, because of its legally accepted authority, is more prone to abuse than ordinary differences. A stronger individual cannot easily use force against a weaker one without opening himself or herself to charges of assault. However, misuse of grading or other student evaluation is relatively difficult to demonstrate insofar as grading relies heavily upon judgment, which the professor has been authorized to make. Thus an offer of sex from a grader is more directly threatening than propositions from other relatively powerful individuals. The ease of misusing discretionary power makes offers by those who wield it similar to propositions in the back alley. Our line of reasoning does condemn other relationships between supervisors and subordinates, insofar as supervisors have power of judgment over employees. However, this implication is not implausible.

It could be objected that it should be possible for professors to explicitly renounce any threat or incentive to the student. A trusted professor and skilled communicator ought to be able to assure the student that she or he may safely refuse an offer. Yet as Dixon (1996) and Davis (1990) argue, although good faith offers may be made, it will be hard for students to know with certainty that a threat is not implicit. Consequently, it will be difficult for the professor to know whether the student's consent is voluntary or results from a (false) understanding of coercion. The professor can ask the student if she or he feels pressured, but the student who senses coercion is likely to sense a need to answer such a question with a false negative. Thus there is no way, even with good intentions and good communication, to ensure that consent is truly voluntary. This gives reason to reject all propositions of sex with students.

In addition to implicit or suspected threats, there is another reason to question the genuineness of student consent to relationships. The faculty-student relationship is one in which the student as a client is under the care of the faculty member and is expected to look up to him or her as an authority. In such relationships, the student may feel a dependence on the faculty member and an excitement and indebtedness regarding their relationship that results in feelings of attraction to the faculty member. Higgins (1998) makes this point in his argument that faculty-student relationships involve a transference love similar to that of psychiatric counselor and patient. He suggests that such a student's attraction to a professor is false, conditioned on the authority inherent in the professor's role and the bond of trust in the shared educational project, and not on rational choice to enter the relationship because of qualities actually possessed by the teacher.

Higgins's argument captures something problematic about faculty-student relationships. One suspects the attraction is not genuine and that the student does not know what she or he is getting into. As Higgins puts it, "when someone is in process, and you have devoted yourself to witnessing and facilitating that process, you are wary to treat as definitive any one version of the evolving being before you" (1998, ¶ 29). This analysis suggests that a faculty member who becomes romantically involved with a student misuses the trust and closeness inherent in his or her role as mentor.

At the same time, aspects of the analogy to the psychiatrist seem overstated. The teaching relationship does not normally involve the intense analysis of personal affairs that the psychiatric relationship does, so it seems less likely that the student would transfer love feelings accidentally to the faculty member. Of course, we would not want to deny that education entails personal growth and excitement. However, whereas immediate personal breakthroughs common in counseling might lead to love feelings, the study of academic material would seem to be sufficiently nonintimate to minimize suspicions of irrational encounters. At the same time, we are wary of defining as voluntary only those relationships which result from a completely accurate and rational understanding of one's mate's virtues. Few relationships could probably satisfy such a demand. While we are skeptical of Higgins's dismissal of faculty-student relationships as uniquely disingenuous, it seems right to say that psychological dynamics in the relationship further call into question both its consensual nature and its value to the participants.

One might wonder if matters are any different if the sexual relationship is initiated by the student instead of the professor. Student initiation would seem to alleviate concerns about coercion, either actual or understood. Indeed, Pichaske (1995) argues that "bans on professor-student relationships are founded on two assumptions," one being that "sex between teachers and students generally is initiated by experienced male professors with naïve female students" (p. B1). He goes on to argue that this assumption is false, as his (seemingly considerable) experience "has been that sexual interaction is more often student-initiated than professor initiated." He goes on to suggest that there is no reason to protect students from relationships that they actively seek. Perhaps faculty should be forbidden from propositioning students but should be free to consent to student propositions of sex or romance.

However, this conclusion is hasty. The distinction between student- and faculty-initiated relationships overemphasizes the origins of the relationship and ignores its continuing nature. A relationship is not something that one consents to once and for all, such that if one entered it freely, we need not worry about that individual's voluntary participation later on. A student may initially enter the relationship freely, but at some point may wish to end the relationship or refuse to engage in all of the activities desired by the professor. To the extent that the student becomes unwilling to engage in the relationship or any aspect of it, coercion of consent again becomes an issue. It is difficult to imagine a romantic relationship in which all encounters and interaction are completely at the suggestion and control of the student. Faculty ought to avoid all sexual involvement with their students, regardless of who makes the first move.

The blanket prohibition we recommend will have the unfortunate result of ruling out relationships entered voluntarily by students who correctly perceived that no threat was being made by the professor. In this sense, the proposed stricture is paternalistic, as it denies some couples the freedom to enter into relationships which they freely choose and view (possibly correctly) as positive for them. Policies against faculty-student romance are in tension with the conception of autonomous individuals that underpins our legal and educational systems.

However, there is reason to single out faculty-student relationships for particular restrictions. We already noted that such relationships are particularly susceptible to an abuse of power which is difficult to monitor or waive. Furthermore, prohibiting faculty-student romance causes little harm or loss of freedom. Because the institutional role relationship between an individual professor and student generally only lasts a short time (e.g., a four-month semester course), little is lost by delaying romantic involvement until after the academic relationship is over. A ban on faculty-student relationships is much less restrictive than bans on interracial, same-sex, or large age-gap relationships, which would permanently thwart intimate contact between groups of individuals. A faculty-student relationship ban only temporarily delays some individuals from enjoying intimate relationships. In return, the ban avoids significant amounts of likely coercion. It also preserves educational integrity, a point that we turn to now.

Faculty-Student Romance and Educational Integrity

While the educational relationship can problematically introduce coercion into the romantic relationship, the romantic relationship can also interfere with the educational process. The most obvious problem with faculty involvement with a student in a class is *favoritism*. A professor is likely to give better grades and recommendations as well as more individual attention to a student with whom he or she is romantically involved. The desire to please and retain a romantic partner and the tendency to want good things for those one cares for makes it likely that a student-lover will be given advantageous treatment. This violates basic norms of educational fairness. The unequal treatment is especially egregious if grades are curved—such that the favored student's success actually hurts other students—but even apart from such a competitive situation, to have one student graded on a different scale than others is unjust. By their nature, grades are comparisons of students, serving to sort them in their access to further educational and employment opportunities. Students and society have a legitimate concern that all are graded equally.

It could be objected that this simply shows that faculty ought not show favoritism, not that they ought not enter relationships with students. After all, faculty will almost inevitably like some students more than others; yet we expect the faculty member to set aside his or her preferences for particular personalities, mannerisms, appearances, and belief systems when it comes to student evaluation. Might faculty not do the same with a romantic partner? Although it may not be impossible to fairly evaluate a romantic partner, it would be very difficult to do so; even if a professor tried, he or she would be unlikely to succeed. Because the faculty member's own happiness and the happiness of his or her loved one is tied to the grade, he or she is likely either to be tempted to break his or her own standards of fairness or to deceive himself or herself into thinking a grade is accurate when it is really influenced by personal interests and attachments. (Additionally, if faculty-student relationships were against university policy and grounds for harassment charges, then the faculty member might favor the student to stay on good terms and avoid such charges.) Thus grading a student with whom one is sexually involved is a conflict of interest.

Dixon (1996) points out that this argument against faculty-student relationships assumes that faculty members are emotionally attached to the students with whom they are sexually involved. It seems not to apply to casual sex with a student, since by definition there would be no attachment (and hence nothing to prevent impartial treatment). This line of argument suggests the seemingly paradoxical conclusion that it is fine for faculty to become sexually involved with students so long as they do not care about them. However, as Dixon notes, sexual relationships almost inevitably create feelings of attachment. Furthermore, even a casual relationship (if enjoyable) would be something that the faculty member would have an interest in maintaining. Almost any imaginable sexual relationship with one's students entails a conflict of interest.

Even if a faculty member succeeded in grading impartially, a romantic involvement with a student would give the *appearance* of unfairness. Other students would think themselves disadvantaged, taking away from the authority of the professor's decisions. The student-lover's own grades and accomplishments would be tarnished for others and perhaps the student would suspect them of being unearned. This compromise of the effectiveness and integrity of the academic process is a reason that faculty should avoid romantic relationships with students. These arguments also imply that faculty ought not teach their own children or other close family members, who they would have a difficult time evaluating impartially. Since universities have an interest in preserving fairness (and its appearance) prohibitions on faculty sexual relations with students in their courses are justified.

In addition to concerns about fairness, there is also another reason to think that faculty-student romance compromises education. Superson (2001) argues that it is difficult for an individual to be both a professor and a lover. A professor is supposed to respond to students' intellectual needs and interests. If the professor is also intimately involved with a student, this is likely to distract from relating to the student as a learner. Crudely, if the professor's mind is on physical intimacy, this may prevent effective instruction. If the professor is relating to students as lovers or potential lovers, class discussion and feedback on student work may be designed to secure and maintain feelings of intimacy rather than promoting student learning. This is one of the reasons romantic relationships are prohibited between therapists and patients: The dual role undermines the therapist's ability to counsel in a way which most benefits the patient. The conflict of interest that suggests unfairness to third parties also ends up being unfair to the student.

It could be objected that a professor might give even more positive and passionate intellectual feedback to his or her student lover. Some academics, particularly women (e.g., Gallop, 1997; Kipnis, 2004), have written of the benefits of their relationships with their professors. The teaching relationship would not seem to be as immediately corrupted by a relationship as would, say, a psychotherapist-client relationship. Therapy, by nature, is supposed to provide objective analysis of an individual's psychological well-being, including her or his sexual and romantic relationships. Thus a therapist involved with a client would be in the impossible role of trying to give impartial counseling about the client's relationship with himself or herself. Professor-student roles would seem to be different insofar as their subject matter is not the student's personal life but some field of general knowledge. Intimacy with the student would not seem to compromise the faculty member's integrity or impartiality in discussing course material (except when the subject of the course includes either faculty-student relationships or romantic relationships). Nevertheless, while it may be possible for academics to succeed in cultivating educationally neutral (or even beneficial) relationships with some students, one suspects that other students propositioned by professors may not be taken seriously, thus depriving them of educational opportunity. The student who is propositioned by the professor is made aware of the physical interest in him or her and may thus feel a loss of recognition as an intellectual being (Superson, 2001).

Furthermore, a pattern of such relationships in which professors regularly proposition students would suggest to students that professors are interested in students more for their bodies than for their minds. And as Superson argues, given that a disproportionate share of such propositions are made by male professors to female students, such actions foster the sexist message that women are to be taken more seriously as sexual than intellectual beings.

Relationships between faculty and students are also likely to disrupt the learning process in the classroom and college. Such relationships lead to gossip, suspicion, and jealousy. This can cause divisiveness in the academic community. This disruption is intensified if the relationship goes badly and members of the community become involved. Tong (1999) notes that such disruption has factored heavily in departmental policies to avoid faculty-student relationships. Although the reactions of others are not a sufficient reason to ban ethical relationships—were community reactions the main problem, it would be incumbent on these third parties to adjust to the otherwise ethical relationship—they are an additional reason to avoid those that are ethically problematic.

Romantic Relationships With University Students Not Taking the Professor's Course

We have argued that professors ought not get involved sexually with students because of the likelihood of both sexual coercion and corruption of education. It is noteworthy that both kinds of argument only apply to students being evaluated or supervised by the professor. On this analysis, it would be appropriate for professors to date and sleep with *former* students as well as other university students not under his or her supervision. Once the student has received a grade and is no longer under the professor's authority, the chance of coercion is gone. It may still be true that the student is attracted to the professor because of the professor's role as an authority and mentor. However, such influences should be reduced now that the student is no longer a regular member of the professor's class. To forbid individuals from entering relationships with anyone who has held a position of authority or status with them would be an excessively paternalistic restriction on individuals' judgment. Again we would be careful about requiring that the attraction behind relationships be uninfluenced by power and status. If we did this, celebrities (much more than academics) would have to be forbidden from engaging in romantic relationships.

Yet relationships with former students can still compromise academic integrity. If professors plan to proposition a student after a course, this may cause bias in grading. A good grade might improve the likelihood of a student welcoming the former professor's advances. Of course, professors should attempt to avoid such partiality just as they should strive to avoid rewarding students who are likely to complain about their grades. However, given the problem of unwitting favoritism as well as the appearance of favoritism when other students see a faculty member dating a former classmate, professors ought to avoid planning relationships with students after a class or propositioning and dating students soon after a course. A policy of rejecting plans to date students will help faculty ensure unbiased grading, maintaining integrity and the appearance of integrity. If a significant time has passed—such that there is little suspicion on the student's, faculty member's, or third party's accounts of biased evaluation—the faculty member might initiate a relationship with a former student.

Some campuses have moved to ban faculty relationships not just with their own students, but with anyone who is a student at the university. Such policies are unnecessary and excessively interfere with personal lives. If the student is not subject to coercion by the faculty member and is not in a position to receive partial treatment, there is little reason to object to the relationship. One might worry that the faculty member is using his or her status as a professor to impress and attract a younger student. There seems to be reason to think that such a faculty member is insecure and the student who becomes involved with him or her is misguided. However, there may be older or relatively mature students with whom a relationship would not be founded on inequality. The student might be a retired professional or employed business professional receiving additional training, and thus the social equal of the professor. Furthermore, as we said above, we cannot require strict social equality or mature motives in all romance. Finally, anyone whom a faculty member is dating or married to may have reason to take university classes and, thus, become a student. A strict ban on faculty-student relationships would force such couples to separate for the duration of study at the professor's institution. Spouses and romantic partners would be denied local access to education, as well as the commonly reduced tuition for families of employees. Prohibitions of intimacy with students not subject to the professor's authority are impractical and unnecessary.

One worry in allowing faculty-student relationships is that the student might later have reason to take the faculty member's course. This is a good reason for faculty to avoid dating anyone who is a major in his or her department or otherwise likely to become his or her student. Otherwise faculty and their student partners should be able to avoid any direct evaluative, supervisory, or authoritative role by the faculty member over the student-lover. It is rare that every student at the university would have to study with a single faculty member. It is possible that a professor involved with a student could find himself or herself serving on a committee to evaluate the student—say, an academic appeals committee. However, it would be possible for the faculty member to simply recuse himself or herself in such situations, avoiding the conflict (as is done by judges who face conflicts of interest). It is excessive to prohibit relationships between adults who are attracted to and find each other's company mutually beneficial on the chance that conflicts requiring ethical judgment might arise in the future.

According to Wagner (1993), at least one university (Christopher Newport) has fired a faculty member after a student complaint about a relationship in which the faculty member had no institutional authority over the student. The student claimed that she suffered emotional trauma after the faculty member terminated the relationship, thus constituting the creation of a hostile educational environment for her. However, as Wagner notes, such a relationship is not legal grounds for sexual harassment. Faculty members do not have a responsibility to ensure nontraumatic personal relationships for all students in the university.

Conservative policies, such as Christopher Newport's, are probably motivated by fear of litigation. Institutions ban all relations—even ethically justified ones—to avoid the possibility of a costly, mistakenly decided lawsuit. Although universities have a legitimate interest in avoiding financial loss, they also have an obligation to avoid unjustifiable restrictions on their faculty and students. Universities ought to be prepared to defend themselves and their employees against invalid suits. The acquiescence of institutional policies in the blanket condemnation of faculty-student relations may have the perverse effect of giving the appearance of legitimacy to spurious complaints of harassment. Furthermore, as Dixon (1996) argues, faculty and students are more likely to observe policies that are ethically defensible. When restrictions are unjustifiably broad, institutions are forced to assert them without rational justification; they become mere authoritarian mandates rather than codes of ethical conduct. Wagner (1993) notes that broad anti sex ual relations policies tend not to be consistently applied, and suggests that in some cases they are used selectively to terminate professors who have lost favor with the university administration. Inconsistency and susceptibility to abuse are additional reasons to avoid overly broad policies.

To recap, university policy is justified in forbidding faculty to be romantically involved with their own students. In addition to committing themselves to such a policy, faculty ought to avoid involvement with anyone who is likely to become their student in the future or who has recently been a student.

Faculty-Student Friendship

According to a popular but superficial understanding of faculty-student relations, as long as faculty don't get sexually involved with their students, there are no problems and anything goes. However, the ethical problems of intimate faculty-student relationships extend beyond sexual fraternization. Although friendships do not evoke the moral suspicion with which our society tends to view sexual relations, friendships between faculty and students raise many of the same questions. Several writers have argued that faculty ought to avoid such friendships. At the same time, others have defended faculty-student friendships and even promoted friendship as the ideal model of an educational relationship.

To assess whether faculty ought to be friends with students, we need a definition of friendship. To be friends with someone is to do more than be *friendly* toward them. It seems that educators should try to be polite, respectful, and caring toward their students just as other professionals engaged in service should be with their clients. Here friendliness is contrasted with rudeness, disrespect, and indifference. Yet it is possible for faculty members to be friendly toward students without becoming friends with them. What, then, is involved in friendship?

Drawing on Aristotle (1985), Markie (1990) defines friends as those who first have a mutual affection for each other as individuals—a fondness which goes beyond a general concern for human well-being. Second, friends share a commitment to assist one another; there is solidarity in friendships. Third, friends share activities—spending time doing things and communicating together. Fourth, friends share information and concerns about each other such that there is a degree of intimacy of mutual knowledge not generally present between mere acquaintances.

It is certainly possible for faculty to become friends with students. They are automatically involved in the shared intellectual process of the classroom. Discussions can carry over outside the classroom, to office hours and informal encounters around campus and town. If faculty and students enjoy each other's company and are concerned to assist each other, this could lead to activities and recreation together outside of the educational context. Students commonly share some personal information about themselves with faculty members. In the process of teaching and advising, faculty may talk about themselves as well. When such personal exchange is mutual another key component of friendship occurs.

Again following Aristotle, Markie (1990) acknowledges that friendship is generally good. Having people about whom one is concerned and with whom one shares activities, information, and assistance is a necessary component of most conceptions of a good, well-lived life. Friendship gives one an opportunity for personal growth, reflection, and enjoyment. On the whole, people are better off the more friends they have. The inherent goodness of friendship provides a reason to think that friendship between faculty and students should be allowed and even encouraged.

Yet friendship with students is potentially open to the same objections as romantic relationships. First, the faculty member might exploit the student friend. Just as it may be difficult to know whether consent to sex is voluntary, it may be difficult to know whether consent to a friendly invitation to coffee, dinner, or a sporting event is voluntary. A student might feel compelled to accept because of concern over his or her grade. Markie (1990) dismisses such concerns by arguing that if the student is not interested, then the two are not really friends. However, the question for faculty members is whether they should try to cultivate and initiate friendships when they may not yet know if the student is a friend. Furthermore, even a true friend may occasionally feel pressured to engage in activities against his or her will. Institutional power can exacerbate this problem.

Perhaps the key point is less that faculty ought not be friends with students than that they ought not make excessive requests of students—friends or otherwise. This is particularly a problem if the faculty member secures the labor of the student-friend, say, research assistance or home repair work. As with faculty-student romance, it will be difficult to determine whether a student agrees to such requests for help as a friend or as a student concerned with his or her grade. If faculty discuss personal needs and burdens with students, the latter may feel pressured to provide emotional concern and support. Clearly faculty should avoid exploiting their institutional power to get people to do things for and spend time with them. However, this seems to imply that faculty ought not ask anything of or initiate personal activities with their students. If followed consistently, it would imply that faculty could not be friends with their students, since friends share activities and personal needs and concerns.

Although we think Markie (1990) and other writers may be too dismissive of such problematic tendencies in faculty-student friendships (and in attempts to cultivate them), we argue that concern over exploitation is not decisive. Rather than eschewing all friendship with students, faculty should simply take measures to try to avoid exploitation. This can be done, in part, by not asking anything of a student-friend that one would not ask and expect of a friend who was not under one's authority. If one would not ask other friends to do one's work without pay, then one should be suspicious of one's interest in asking a student to do so. However, if the faculty member asks the student to do something that is normal in casual friendships, such as having coffee or help moving a piece of furniture, it would not seem to be exploitative. (A difficult question is the line between friendship and romance. At some point, personal interest and requests for shared activities suggests romantic interest rather than friendship. The desire to avoid any appearance of sexual harassment is surely reason for faculty to avoid pursuing friendship with students. However, we point out that offers can be made in a manner such that there would be no reason to suspect sexual coercion.) In most cases, students welcome faculty offers of association. The advice to not make any unwanted offers seems generally sound, but as Kipnis (2004) points out, it suffers from a near paradox: How does one know if the other party is interested until one asks? Nevertheless there is a general obligation on the part of those holding power to avoid making offers and requests that one suspects others would not be interested in without the factor of the gradebook. Faculty forays into friendship can also be protected from suspicion of exploitation insofar as they include assurances that the student may refuse.

Of course, it will be noted that we rejected such an argument as a defense of sexual offers and relations. However, there are important differences. Students have much less reason to fear that spurning a friendship offer will lead to faculty retaliation. Furthermore, individuals are much less likely to try to force a friendship with a less-than-willing partner than a sexual relationship. Friendship lacks reward when the other party is uninterested. Finally, most pressure lacks the extreme violation of sexual coercion. Sex involves a greater physical intimacy than most activities and, for most individuals, has a psychological and symbolic connection to personal identity. Coercing a person to engage in sex is a much greater violation than pressuring her or him to have coffee, play tennis, or go to dinner. Of course, nobody ought to be forced to do the latter either. However, there is less need to avoid all risk of coercion regarding such forms of association and activity. It is enough to ask faculty to exercise care and judgment in avoiding pressure in their dealings with students as friends and associates.

Friendship and Equal Treatment

The central concern in faculty-student friendships is less coercion of friendship by instructor power than corruption of teaching by friendship. In short, the concern is that there is favoritism toward friends. Cahn (1986) suggests that the fundamental principle of equitable treatment will automatically be violated by faculty-student friendships: "If one student in a seminar is invited to the professor's home for dinner, then all should receive invitations" (p. 36). From this perspective, insofar as friendship involves a relationship and activities that will not be shared with all students, it is an illegitimate form of favoritism.

Yet as Jackson and Hagen (2001) counter, Cahn gives too wide a scope to the demand of equity. The professor owes equitable treatment in the performance of his or her duties of teaching, grading, and advising, but does not owe rigid equality of treatment outside of this professional role. If the professor was neighbor to a student, the professor might occasionally help the student jump-start his or her car without incurring an obligation to give similar assistance to everyone in the class. Similarly, it seems that a professor might go out to coffee and become friends with some students because he or she gets along better with them than others.

The case against faculty-student friendships is not that granting friendship to one, but not others, is wrongful discrimination. Rather, the main concern is that friendship with the professor will give some students an advantage in the classroom. That is, the friend of the professor will be given more learning opportunities, such as discussing class material over coffee breaks, meals, and recreational outings. Furthermore the faculty member may give his or her friend preferential grading. It is this propensity to discriminate in favor of one's friends that is the cornerstone of Markie's (1990) argument against faculty-student friendship. He makes the case that even well-meaning professors are inevitably going to favor their friends because of the nature of friends sharing activities and concerns with each other. Second, friends are generally inclined (if not obligated) to do favors for each other, such that faculty will be pushed to give unearned grades to friends. Markie concludes that to maintain equal treatment of students and avoid a conflict of interest in which unjustifiable bias is likely, professors ought to avoid forming friendships with students. Just as judges and juries could not be thought capable to serve impartially in a trial of their friends, teachers could not grade a friend equitably.

Markie (1990) goes on to argue that faculty can and should take measures to avoid becoming friends with students. Professors can withhold personal information and refrain from engaging in leisure activities with students. By keeping the relationship focused on academics, faculty will prevent the development of bonds of friendship that otherwise might form. Markie explicitly endorses professional "distance"—avoiding personal, familiar, intimate, or playful encounters with students. The restriction on intimacy also serves to prevent heightened responsiveness to individual concerns and needs, such as making exceptions to class policies.

Beyond this argument for equity, one might argue that avoiding friendship and maintaining distance helps to preserve the educational focus of the faculty-student relationship. One of the greatest pitfalls of friendship with students is that the faculty member will treat courses as leisure activities, such that classroom discussion degrades into unfocused chat. If the professor loses distance and becomes regarded as a peer in the classroom, he or she may lose student respect and the authority to lead the class.

Conditional Defense of Faculty-Student Friendship

Although Markie's arguments raise important concerns about faculty-student friendship, we think they fail to show that all such relationships are wrong. The concerns about favoritism and a loss of commitment to education and classroom authority are potential hazards of friendship with students, but are not inherent in it.

The idea that friends would wrongly be given additional educational opportunities has been countered by Jackson and Hagen (2001). They argue that additional learning opportunities are not to be regretted. If a student bumped into a faculty member around campus or town, it would not be inappropriate for the faculty member to answer questions about class material, even though this will give one student a form of contact not had by others. Some students will always be more able to meet with and ask questions of faculty because their schedules, energy, and personalities make it easier for them; these students will gain advantages lost by others. The faculty member is not unfair in meeting with these students so long as he or she provides educational opportunities for others to use if they see fit. The faculty member should make office hours available and be flexible in agreeing to meet with students, such that any student could get extra discussion time with the professor. To guarantee that no student received more assistance than any other would require the faculty member reducing assistance to the least common denominator—the amount secured by the most harried, overworked, and uncommitted student; the faculty member would have to give essentially no assistance to anyone in the name of fairness. Contrary to this, as long as access is given to any who seek it, the faculty member has provided equity. If some make better use of this time or are more able to meet the faculty member outside of class, this is not to be regretted.

On the other hand, it is true that the faculty member ought not give advantages in assessment to friends. In meeting with them casually, the professor should not give them preparation for exams that would not be made available to other students; this provides an opportunity denied to others by policy, resulting in formal inequality. Likewise, the faculty member is responsible for grading and assessing all students fairly, including friends. Of course, the possibility of this is exactly what Markie

(1990) denies. In response, Jackson and Hagen (2001) argue, first, that friends do not owe favoritism to friends. Friendship is not a contract in which we promise particular, much less unbounded, assistance. Friends assist each other out of concern, but they are not obligated to (and indeed should not) assist one another in breaking moral rules. Rather, Jackson and Hagen argue, friendship can be tailored to the situations in which we find ourselves. In a professional setting, one does not expect special treatment from or casual conversation with one's friend. So two soldiers might be friends while remaining bound to follow orders and pursue their mission regardless of concern for each other's well-being. If friends can place rules over personal ties in life-and-death situations, one might expect that faculty could set aside friendship in grading.

Indeed, the logic of Markie's argument implies that there should never be any friendships in the workplace, at least between superiors and those they evaluate. Indeed Markie (1990) bites the bullet and accepts that tenured faculty ought not befriend tenure-track professors whom they will eventually evaluate for tenure and full professors ought not befriend those of lower rank whom they will evaluate for promotion. Such restrictions, if not absurd, are at least a high price to pay for some advantages in fairness in evaluation. When people work together for years in close quarters, it is natural for some friendship to develop. Workplace friendships, which mix elements of recreation and personal interaction with work, make jobs more enjoyable and enriching. It seems unfortunate to take joy out of work by denying such friendships. Furthermore, as Jackson and Hagen (2001) aver, drawing these boundaries results in a kind of caste system in which people only associate with those at their own status. This risks losing communication, understanding, and solidarity between those in different positions. Of course, professors cannot be required to develop friendships at all levels, since friendship cannot be forced or chosen at will. But for the most part, friendships within and across ranks develop of their own course and contribute to the academy's functioning.

Students can be viewed as junior colleagues in the learning process. Graduate students and advanced undergraduates may be working closely with faculty as research or teaching assistants. When there are such shared projects, interests, goals, and challenges, friendship will be particularly difficult to avoid. Strict adherence to the ideal of distance will seem unnatural and may limit the amount of understanding, communication, and enjoyment that can be gained from the learning and teaching process. Nor is friendship only inevitable and beneficial for graduate students and assistants. Faculty may also have reason to make acquaintances outside the classroom with students, including undergraduates. Faculty may find themselves working and recreating with students in campus clubs, off-campus associations, and volunteer activities. To prohibit friendships in such an environment is to deny a potentially positive relationship to each individual in order to maintain an artificial distance.

Whether instructor distance, with its seriousness and lack of personal exchange, is valuable in education has been questioned by Tom (1997). She argues that instructors firmly withholding personal information in the name of maintaining an air of professional distance does more harm than good, erecting a barrier between professor and student that limits education. Professors' personal references and revelations can be useful in providing living examples of issues discussed in the classroom. Revealing a professor's humanity and individuality can be instructive and help students relate to their professor. Tom argues that while one can (and sometimes should) be personal as a professor, one should retain awareness of power relationships. This means not allowing personal sharing on the part of the instructor to become a dogmatic imposition of views or appeal for student assistance. Because personal sharing can lead to complications of power, coercion, and favoritism, distance is a tempting solution. However, it comes at considerable cost.

Furthermore, it's not clear that distance resolves the problem of favoritism. No matter how distant a professor is he or she will like some students more than others. Some individuals will strike the professor as brighter, wittier, more decent, and generally more likeable than others. No normal human being is able to completely shut off all emotional response and maintain a completely neutral attitude toward the people she encounters. The challenge of the teaching professional is to avoid letting these inevitable personal feelings prejudice the education one provides.

Jackson and Hagen (2001) counter Markie's analogy of educators and judges, arguing that law is different insofar as it involves definite winners and losers. Judge and jury should not be friends of either plaintiff or defendant because they will tend to side with one over the other. But a professor need not take a side. Jackson and Hagen suggest that professors are more like doctors, who try to benefit everyone they serve. We do not worry about a doctor befriending one patient because there is no reason to think this will lessen his or her commitment to others. Similarly, a professor can be friends with some students and still do his or her best to educate the rest.

Nonetheless, in some respects Markie's analogy holds more than Jackson and Hagen's. Professors do have to evaluate students. And although students are not as directly pitted against one another as adversaries in a trial, in a sense students are competing for scarce goods. If grades are curved, they are in direct competition. If a high score sets the curve or takes one of a limited quota of As, then a high score for the professor's friend harms others. A professor grading a friend would probably have some temptation to score the friend highly, just as the professor grading a child or spouse. In medicine there is generally no such thing as too-good care, but in education there is such a thing as grading too high and giving too many breaks. Perhaps one could argue that undeserved grades are really bad for the recipient, just as too much medication may be bad for the patient. Thus, favoritism would harm one's friend and be totally irrational! However, such an argument gets implausible when the friend is competing to get into medical school, finish his or her dissertation, or receive a glowing letter of recommendation. Some grades and evaluations lead fairly directly to external goods, namely opportunities for positions with good pay and social recognition, such that an undeserved positive evaluation is of benefit—or is at least likely to be viewed as such to both the student and his or her professor-friend.

Furthermore, while Jackson and Hagen are right to say that favoritism is a problem whether instructors befriend students or not, friendship would seem to worsen the problem. Carrying out those activities unique to friendship (i.e., spending personal time and exchanging personal information with students) is likely to increase professors' sympathetic feeling toward them as individuals beyond anything felt for students the professor lacks personal involvement with. Developing a friendship adds to the difficulty of maintaining equitable assessment— something similar (to a lesser degree) to being romantically involved with a student. Furthermore, even if a professor maintains equity while teaching a student-friend, friendship tends to give the *appearance* of a conflict of interest and favoritism. Any student known to be a friend of the instructor would be suspected of undeserved advantages. If the faculty member warmly jokes with one student before or after class, other students may feel discriminated against—taking away from the faculty member's authority in the classroom, regardless of how impartial the professor is in the formal assigning of grades and writing of letters of recommendation.

We acknowledge that friendships with students pose an ethical challenge for faculty. Yet though not susceptible to complete dissolution, the arguments against them are not decisive. Faculty can cultivate friendships while working to maintain objectivity in the grading process. If a faculty member questions whether he or she can grade a friend objectively, then he or she has an obligation to either pull back from the friendship or to ensure that the friend in question not take his or her class. In the conduct of the class itself, faculty can allay suspicions of inequity and envy by treating the friend similarly to the other students. The friendship should be kept separate from the class environment to remind educator and student of the need for impartiality and to forestall the loss of faculty authority in the classroom.

Although faculty must retain a professional demeanor of seriousness and equitable treatment in the conduct of the course, we think Cahn and Markie's endorsement of distance is overstated and that the approaches of Jackson/Hagen and Tom are closer to the mark. Faculty can avoid letting education dissolve into frivolous play without resistance of all intimate sharing. It is appropriate for faculty to discuss personal matters with students if they choose, if this is relevant to course material, and if this in no way is done to put a burden on or pressure students to do something for the faculty member. Furthermore, faculty should encourage students who are interested in sharing their own personal concerns over issues such as personal goals, relationships, priorities, and health. Discussion with the experienced and respected faculty member can be of assistance to the student. It is true that faculty are not trained as counselors, are not necessarily prepared to become personal advisors and confidants, and could not possibly do this with all of their students. However, there is reason to think that instructors contribute the most to students when they are able to show interest and concern for the student's whole personhood. The current pre-occupation with policing faculty intimacy with students has the unfortunate effect of dissuading positive and caring faculty involvement in students' lives, a loss bemoaned by more than a few commentators (e.g., Baker, 1996; Benton, 2004; Hopkins-Powell, 2002; Tom, 1997).

Discussions or shared activities outside of class may occasion the development of faculty-student friendship. In some cases, such as those in which faculty and student work together on an educational project or are involved in extracurricular activities, friendship will tend to develop naturally. This need not be resisted, so long as the faculty member ensures that there is no coercion and does not promise any favoritism will be given to the student in the classroom. There would rarely be any reason for a faculty member to attempt to develop a friendship with an undergraduate taking a single course from him or her. If the two share some interest (e.g., tennis, politics, or fishing), they could wait to take it up after the semester is over, and there is little reason to complicate the relationship by taking it up during the course.

However, in the case of a graduate student or major in the faculty member's department, the two may know each other so well and work together so much for so long that it would be a great restriction to ask them to wait indefinitely to become friends. In other cases, a faculty member might already be friends with undergraduate or graduate students who sign up for his or her class. The faculty member might suggest that friends take the class with another professor to avoid the complications of favoritism. If the friend has a reason for taking the faculty member's course—either because there are no other instructors, convenient sections, or options that are as interesting—it is permissible for the professor to accept a friend in class. The professor would be obligated to take pains to avoid favoritism. Even the destabilizing appearance of favoritism should be minimized by avoiding shows of affection and attachment to one's friend in the classroom and around other students.

In any case, "friendship" is not an easily definable legal category that could serve as the basis of policy. Thus, universities should eschew any attempts to regulate faculty-student friendship. Placing reasonable limits on such relationships is the responsibility of individual faculty members.

Friendship and the Ideal Faculty-Student Relationship

The discussion of faculty-student relationships does well to note not simply the boundary conditions, that which is forbidden, but also those ideal forms of relating to students for which faculty ought to strive. In this vein, we noted that some writers recommend faculty-student friendship not only as permissible but also as an ideal model of the educational relationship (e.g., Baker, 1996; Hendley, 1978). Since Plato it has been noted that the pursuit of knowledge can be the basis for friendship. Plato's teacher Socrates, who remains the hero of and ideal model for subsequent educators, cultivated and enjoyed friendship with his students. His personal decisions and concerns frequently served as the basis for their mutual philosophical inquiry. The openly intimate and passionately engaged communication characteristic of friendship can increase the potential of shared inquiry, yielding greater education.

Friendship also involves a form of caring that is conducive to beneficent relations with the other. Friends do not view each other as objects to be manipulated to serve individualistic ends. Rather, they encounter the other as another self, who must be understood and related to on his or her own terms. Thus the friendship is, as Hendley (1978) explains, the paradigm case of what Martin Buber called an I—Thou (as opposed to I—it) relationship. Similarly, when teaching is done well it does not manipulate students to some predetermined endpoint. The ideal educator responds to the selfhood of the student, taking seriously his or her independent and individual needs and perspectives.

Buber himself thought that although teaching shared friendship's I—Thou status, the former differed significantly from the latter. He argued that teaching is a one-way activity such that the instructor takes seriously students and contributes to their individual growth, but that the student does not respond to or contribute to the individuality of the instructor. As commentators such as Hendley reply, Buber seems to overlook the ability of students to respond to their professors as individuals and influence the professor—particularly at the university level. Ideally, professors learn along with students. Students are not formally responsible for instructing the professor; yet if education goes well, such that students and faculty are both engaged, this can and should happen.

Although teaching can involve reciprocal sharing of information, enjoyment in a shared learning activity, and sharing of personal information, we think that it should be acknowledged that friendship is not a necessary goal or practicable ideal in education. First, it is simply impossible for professors to be friends with all or even most students. Professors will not like all students and will not be able to cultivate solidarity with all of them. Friendship requires time and personal intimacy, things not allowed by the size of modern classrooms and the pace of education. The pressure to cover material required for standardized exams, academic advancement, and certification reduces time for unconstrained discussion. Unlike Socrates, modern educators do not get to choose their students, and they must give them impartial grades. The circumstances and duties of university education today make friendship with students much less feasible and more perilous for contemporary educators than it was for their classic forbearers.

Furthermore, it would be harmful to attempt to push friendship on either student or educator. Students ought not be expected to like and openly share personal matters with all of their professors. Educators should be open to such student communication but should not press students to engage in it. Students may choose other confidants and friends if they wish. Similarly, professors ought not be pushed to be open and playful with their students. Though some openness is effective for many professors, it will feel too familiar (and hence be unnatural) to others.

Teaching can be good, even excellent, without friendship. Educators must show caring and understanding for students' learning, well-being, and independence. Similarly, teaching excellence requires passion in the pursuit of knowledge and an effort to relate material to real life. Educators do well to introduce humor and playfulness into the exploration of course material. However, a professor can bring concern and passion to a course without inviting the intimacy and open-ended solidarity and interaction involved in friendship. And the professor can give real examples and tell jokes without inviting the depth and extent or personal exchange that friends share. Engaged teaching will probably at times lead to friendship with students. As we have said, this is to be treated carefully but not necessarily regretted and avoided.

Conclusion

Our discussion of faculty-student relationships has led to the following suggestions:

1) In dealing with faculty-student romantic relationships:
   - Faculty ought to avoid romantic and sexual involvement with their students or those likely to become their students in the near future. University policy is justified in prohibiting this.
   - Those with whom faculty are sexually involved or to whom they are intimately related should not take the faculty member's courses or otherwise be evaluated by the faculty member.
   - Faculty ought to avoid seeking relationships with students too soon after completion of a course.
   - Faculty may become involved with university students not likely to take the faculty member's course or students who previously studied with the professor.

2) In dealing with faculty-student friendships:
   - No prohibitions on friendship are necessary. Faculty-student friendships are in principle acceptable.
   - Faculty should avoid all coercion or semblance of coercion in suggesting shared activities with or making requests of students.
   - Faculty must strive for equity in evaluation, regardless of friendship.
   - Faculty should avoid displays of particular affection for friends in the classroom and should maintain a professional atmosphere, no matter how many friends are present.
   - Faculty ought to strive for interactions with students which are caring, respectful, emotionally engaged, relevant to life, and enjoyable. However, this does not require the open-ended sharing of activities and personal lives involved in friendship.

Conclusion

We have argued for an array of obligations in university teaching. If these arguments are on the mark, then teaching is a moral enterprise and the responsibilities of faculty members are considerable. In discussing most of these obligations, we have rarely called for more restrictive rules on the professorate. Formal policy requirements and punitive measures are only justifiable in cases of egregious breaches of clear rules. For example, universities may justifiably punish faculty who become sexually involved with their students, clearly discriminate against students for reasons not relevant to coursework, devote significant amounts of class time to matters unrelated to the course subject, or regularly skip class.

Laws and university policies are not suitable means for addressing most ethical concerns in college teaching, such as the fairness of grades, the appropriateness of assignments, the amount of energy dedicated to course preparation, or the quality of faculty relationships with students. This is in part because the definitions of fairness, effectiveness, sufficiency, and relationship quality are themselves contested by experts and if not utterly subjective, they at least allow significant room for discretionary judgment. It would be impossible to formulate any specific rules about what faculty must achieve in these areas. Any specification of minimal amounts of time spent preparing for class, talking to students, or grading assignments would be arbitrary and ill-suited to some situations. Attempts to enforce good teaching practice would be counterproductive, unnecessarily restrictive, and result in unjustifiable sanctions of faculty.

Additionally, the policing of teaching methods endangers academic freedom by coercing lesson construction and student interaction to demonstrate compliance with policies. The legal stifling of independent course planning would reduce student access to diverse views, which could be censored by either overly broad institutional interpretation of policy or by faculty fear thereof. The depth of inquiry and intellectual debate would likely be reduced by the regulation of teaching practice.

For example, a state law requiring that faculty give balanced instruction about any controversial topic under consideration would be harmful insofar as it would likely encourage faculty to either avoid controversial topics or be pushed to include an array of views that the faculty member considered less than worthwhile. Similar points apply to rules against unnecessary obscenity, familiarity with students, and objectivity in grading practices. Such policies would interfere with not only flawed but legitimate teaching methods but also innovative and effective practices. The enforcement of teaching regulations detracts from, rather than fosters, faculty understanding of teaching as a moral endeavor in which professors seek to contribute to student development and inquiry.

Although further incursions against academic freedom in the name of "enforcing ethics" are to be resisted, this does not mean that academic ethics should be resisted. Because teaching does not lend itself to external regulation, instructors have a particular duty to observe ethical principles in their teaching. Following ethical purposes and moral obligations is not restrictive of individual autonomy, but rather a necessary correlative of it. As Immanuel Kant (that original defendant of the moral supremacy of the principle of autonomy) makes clear, freedom's true meaning is self-government according to principles derived from one's own reason, not doing whatever one feels. Although some range of teaching styles are legitimate, not all teaching decisions are matters of personal preference. There are better and worse choices in teaching.

Although schools should not attempt to require any conception of objectivity in grading, friendliness in relationship with students, or balance in coverage of course material, we have argued that professors have an obligation to strive for these things. Grading can be arbitrary, relationships with students disrespectful and insufficiently caring, and class presentation can be unbalanced and indoctrinating. Faculty can and should avoid, or at least minimize, such ethical problems. Positively, faculty ought to prepare quality, balanced lectures and treat students respectfully, caringly, and equally.

The responsibilities of professors are magnified because of the power which they hold over students through the gradebook. There is a particular duty to use this authority well and refrain from abusing it. Professors have a captive, relatively impressionable audience in their students, and they have an obligation to use this opportunity for positive influence without indoctrination.

Systemic Obstacles to Ethical Teaching

As we said in the introduction, some faculty will deny that ethical advice is necessary—asserting that faculty as a matter of course are aware of their responsibilities and inclined to fulfill them. However, we suspect that such claims to inerrancy are overstated. We have shown that teaching involves ethical dilemmas that can be difficult to sort out for even the intelligent and well-intentioned. Although faculty may know (in principle) how to act, contexts may arise in which pressures and conflicts invite rash conduct. Professors committed in principle to teaching well cut corners to finish other projects. Faculty who generally respect students may find themselves slipping into denigration when they are frustrated by slow progress, disruptions, uninformed questions, or repugnant views.

Pressures to unethical conduct are exacerbated by unfortunate trends in institutions of higher education. A primary threat to faculty ethics is simply the time pressure involved in university teaching. The drive to cut costs and raise revenues has led to increases in average class size and faculty course loads. With more classes to teach, papers to grade, and students to advise, professors have less time to dedicate to each student. Such pressures are a major cause of practices relating to lack of faculty preparation for courses, poor assignment construction, and reliance upon multiple-choice testing. Time pressures on faculty may indirectly contribute to other educational problems, such as poorer relationships with students. Greater teaching obligations leave instructors less able to get to know and relate to students as individuals. The time crunch can lead to faculty resentment of student needs and cause professors to view their pupils as obstacles, rather than opportunities for education.

While faculty teaching demands have increased, there has been no reduction in expectations of scholarly production. On the contrary, the publication requirements for tenure and promotion have risen in recent years, encouraged by the fierce competition for open academic positions. While this means that today's professors have curriculum vitae impressively filled with publications and accomplishments, these same luminaries face greater pressures and have less time for students. Many universities have also moved to reduce faculty release time, cutting sabbaticals for faculty development and research. Because at most institutions, especially state universities, salaries have not increased proportionally to those in the private sector, many faculty teach during the summer and take on extra loads during the school year to help support themselves and their families. For overworked faculty, exhortations to a greater ethical commitment to teaching—without reward or institutional support—are a hard sell. Professors may be simply unable or, lacking institutional support, unwilling to devote greater energy to the quality of their teaching and relationships with students.

The challenge to faculty ethics is worsened by the growing use of temporary, adjunct faculty. Such employees normally work several jobs to make ends meet, meaning that they have even less time for students. Furthermore, since they lack long-term attachment to institutions and departments and receive small rewards, adjunct faculty are likely to have less commitment to providing a quality education and serving their institutions. It might be argued that the permanent threat of release which temporary faculty face ought to give them more incentive to teach effectively and serve their departments and colleges diligently. Anybody familiar with higher education will be able to think of some new, young adjunct instructors who bring both more energy and ability to relate to students than many tenured faculty. Nonetheless, this energy and dedication is something that few are able to keep up for long under conditions of low pay and lack of reciprocal institutional commitment.

Current trends of higher teaching workloads, greater research expectations, and a shift to temporary faculty undermine faculty ability to carry through with obligations to students and to reflect on their ethical duties. To foster the conditions in which our ethical recommendations can be realized, we must also endorse university policies of maintaining manageable course loads and research expectations, opportunities for sabbaticals and other release time for faculty development, and use of primarily tenure-track as opposed to temporary instructors.

Although reasonable workloads and institutional support of faculty are important components of promoting integrity in teaching, they are not sufficient. The mere freeing up of faculty time will not necessarily lead to its use for ethical reflection and student service. If teaching ethics is to be retained, much less strengthened, faculty will have to devote energy to the analysis and improvement of their teaching practices and relationships with students. As we have already rejected institutional requirements regarding teaching styles as violating academic freedom, the question arises—how can this be done? Faculty are notoriously resistant to ethical training, both because of its demand on their time and its seeming imputation of their immorality. Faculty may see even the suggestion that they should take things such as sexual harassment prevention, sensitivity to difference, or fairness in grading more seriously as an incursion into their academic freedom.

However, universities can hold faculty-development workshops and forums for the discussion of ethical issues in teaching without contravening academic freedom. Even requiring attendance at ethics programs would not necessarily impinge on intellectual freedom, so long as individual academics were free to choose what to make of and how to implement the ideas discussed. However, given that required learning opportunities tend to be met with resistance and result in less engagement than those that are optional, we would recommend forums on ethical issues in teaching advertised as presenting alternative views and inviting faculty participation.

Faculty ethics may also be fostered by faculty mentoring programs in which senior faculty share experience with and answer questions of junior faculty. In the independent (and sometimes lonely) teaching profession, new professors benefit from having an individual to approach with ethical questions besides the department chair—who provides his or her primary tenure and promotion review. Discussions with a mentor, who provides experience without being a direct supervisor, can help new faculty members clear up their questions as they arise. Such opportunities for assistance with concrete problems can be more helpful than general sessions on ethics that are abstracted from professors' actual academic lives. Being pushed to reflect on their teaching practice might have positive results for senior faculty as well.

Finally, ethical issues in teaching ought to be introduced in graduate education. As many commentators have pointed out, it is surprising that graduate programs say as little as they do about the nature and challenges of the profession that their students are preparing to enter. Talking about the ethics of teaching in graduate courses would be beneficial not only for future employers of new faculty, but also for the students themselves—who could be more prepared for the dilemmas that inevitably arise in their new jobs. Many graduate programs oppose such practical course-work because it is seen as lacking the academic rigor of other disciplinary material. However, ethical issues raise many important and complex intellectual questions which make them worthy of graduate study and credit in their own right, separate from their practical benefits to students and society. Furthermore, discussions of fair and effective grading practices, the extent of legitimate advocacy, and the nature of indoctrination demand participants to reflect on the status of knowledge in their disciplines. Understanding of such debates and development of their own reasoned perspectives on them is of no small educational value to students mastering a field and preparing to teach it to others.

If ethical conduct in teaching is to receive consistent attention, faculty will have to accept that their jobs have ethical import and that they can benefit from personal reflection and dialogue with others on these issues. Support from institutions and other faculty will help foster engagement with ethics. Of course, in the final analysis, whatever the commitment of institutions and faculties as bodies to ethics, ethical teaching will depend upon the judgment and integrity of individual faculty members.

Grounds of Faculty Ethical Commitment

If the ultimate foundation of ethical faculty conduct and sanction for unethical conduct is the conscience of the individual faculty member, we should consider the prospects for the development of and adherence to professorial conscience. Thus we close by asking why faculty ought to be concerned to follow the moral principles we have laid out. Inquiries into the question about the motive for ethics beg a first response that morality is simply what one should do. Asking "Why should I be moral?" is in a sense asking "Why should I do what I should do?" which is question begging. Other personal motives not only are not required for moral conduct but also would seem to detract from its moral purity.

However, from another perspective it makes sense to give additional reasons to be moral. Educators, like other individuals, may find it difficult to motivate themselves to do that which they know they ought to do. Like everyone else, professors have commitments other than professional ethics—such as individual self-interest and furthering the well-being of family, country, or political or religious causes—which are in principle legitimate and may conflict with the moral demands on them as professors. If we are to show that our moral suggestions can be followed by real professors and succeed in giving these individuals reason to follow them, we do well to note personal rewards in ethical teaching.

A first motive for moral conduct is simply individual integrity. A life is better lived if lived according to principles held as important. A life of self-interest, in which principles are not pursued for their own sake, is considered a shallow and incomplete life. For most, the violation of one's own principles results in inner conflicts which ultimately are unhealthy and undermine personal happiness. Somewhat paradoxically, individuals appear to be happier when they do not adopt the egoistic aim of maximizing self-interest. Rather, happiness is a byproduct of a life in which other goals are pursued for their intrinsic worth separate from self-interest.

Beyond the personal value of integrity, faculty have particular motives for adhering to ethical conduct in their profession, even when there is no threat of external sanction. Academics are generally committed to the pursuit of knowledge and have a personal stake in its encouragement. Rigorous, effective, and fair teaching and evaluation promote the process of inquiry, and are thereby of interest to faculty regardless of their formal duties to others. Although a single well-prepared lesson, fairly treated student, or individually counseled advisee makes a minute contribution to the spread of human knowledge, actively pursuing and contributing (in however small a way) to this ultimate goal is of intrinsic value to most who choose an academic career.

Finally, as citizens of their state and the world, professors have an interest in (and normally a concerned commitment to) the fostering of civic life and democratic politics. Intellectuals have a particular responsibility for the quality of political discussion and community understanding. Their commitment to the process of inquiry and the pursuit of knowledge and understanding implies a concern for civic dialogue. This gives faculty an additional motivation to teach students effectively and, just as importantly, in a manner that fosters their participation as citizens. This can be done, in part, by teaching ethical principles as they arise in course subjects. Perhaps more importantly, professors teach democratic deliberation through modeling it. A professor's fairness, humaneness, and benevolence in dealing with students can influence the latter's patterns of social interaction and intellectual discussion. When discussing divisive issues, if professors can retain respect for students, give balanced presentations of conflicting arguments, refrain from dogmatism and indoctrination in their advocacy, and be charitable in entertaining objections, they serve as positive models for social and political inquiry. Outside of academia, students are subjected to models of political discourse characterized by dogmatism, manipulation, irrational persuasion by ad hominem and red herring arguments, and appeals to emotion and force. If we are to have principled alternatives to the forms of political debate presented by the *O'Reilly Factor* and the talking points of political parties, academics must provide them. As intellectuals, professors have a professional and personal interest in fair and rational deliberation. Although the actions of individual faculty members are unlikely to be of great social influence, engagement in and contribution to the democratic process is of intrinsic value to most faculty.

Educational professionals are committed, at least in part, to John Dewey's (1897) early statement of education's potential:

> I believe that education is the fundamental method of social progress and reform. All reforms which rest simply upon the law, or the threatening of certain penalties, or upon changes in mechanical or outward arrangements, are transitory and futile. . . . But through education society can formulate its own purposes, can organize its own means and resources, and thus shape itself with definiteness and economy in the direction in which it wishes to

move. . . . Education thus conceived marks the most perfect and intimate union of science and art conceivable in
human experience. (pp. 9–10)

If this statement strikes us as overly optimistic, and perhaps potentially
dangerous in its hopes for social improvement through education, it is
because it fails to develop education's commitment to democratic discourse and autonomous inquiry. Dewey (1916/1966) emphasizes precisely these themes later in *Democracy and Education*, when he states that
his discussion of education had heretofore

assumed that the aim of education is to enable individuals
to continue their education—or that the object and
reward of learning is continued capacity for growth. Now
this idea cannot be applied to all the members of a society
except where intercourse of man with man is mutual, and
except where there is adequate provision for the recon-
struction of social habits and institutions by means of
wide stimulation arising from equitably distributed interests. And this means a democratic society. (p. 100)

This belief that a democratic process characterized by open inquiry
respectful of the development and rights of individuals will lead to social
improvement underpins the ethical purpose of teaching.

   If these arguments are right, the ethical obligations which face faculty should not be perceived solely as restrictions constraining faculty conduct from the outside (although they are at least this). Deep personal and
professional commitments make the realization of ethical teaching highly desirable to most professors, separate from any institutional or social
sanctions of unethical conduct.

   Of course, the fact that faculty have motives to be ethical does not
mean that they will always follow them. At times faculty will fail to recognize their greater calling or have other conflicting motives. However,
the existence of such motives to be ethical gives us reason to expect that
faculty can dedicate themselves to the guidelines we have suggested. For
the skeptical it may give reasons to engage in the continuing project of
formulating and acting on a defensible ethic of teaching.

Bibliography

Ackerman, F. (1996). Be reasonable and do it my way: Advocacy in the college classroom. In P. M. Spacks (Ed.), *Advocacy in the classroom: Problems and possibilities* (pp. 283–292). New York, NY: St. Martin's Press.

Amada, G. (1999). *Coping with misconduct in the college classroom: A practical model.* Ashville, NC: College Administration Publications.

Anderson, C. W. (1989). The role of education in the academic disciplines in teacher education. In A. E. Woolfork (Ed.), *Research perspectives on the graduate preparation of teachers* (pp. 88–107). Englewood Cliffs, NJ: Prentice Hall.

Anderson, R. S., & Speck, B. W. (Eds.). (1998). *New directions for teaching and learning: No. 74. Changing the way we grade student performance: Classroom assessment and the new learning paradigm.* San Francisco, CA: Jossey-Bass.

Andrews, J., Garrison, D. R., & Magnusson, K. (1996). The teaching and learning transaction in higher education: A study of excellent professors and their students. *Teaching in Higher Education, 1*(1), 81–103.

Angelo, T. A., & Cross, K. P. (1993). *Classroom assessment techniques: A handbook for college teachers* (2nd ed.). San Francisco, CA: Jossey-Bass.

The Associated Press. (2005). *Anti-creationism prof quits department chair.* Retrieved October 16, 2006, from: http://archives.econ.utah.edu /archives/marxism/2005w49/msg00217.htm

Aristotle. (1985). *Nicomachean ethics* (T. Irwin, Trans.). Indianapolis, IN: Hackett Publishing Company.

Bain, K. (2004). *What the best college teachers do.* Cambridge, MA: Harvard University Press.

Baiocco, S. A., & DeWaters, J. N. (1998). *Successful college teaching: Problem-solving strategies of distinguished professors.* Old Tappan, NJ: Allyn & Bacon.

Baker, E. (1982). The specification of writing tasks. *Evaluation in Education, 5*(3), 291–297.

Baker, R. L. (1996). The ethics of faculty-student friendships. In L. Fisch (Ed.), *Ethical dimensions of college and university teaching: Understanding and honoring the special relationship between teachers and students* (pp. 25–32). San Francisco, CA: Jossey-Bass.

Banta, T. W., Lund, J. P., Black, K. E., & Oblander, F. W. (1996). *Assessment in practice: Putting principles to work on college campuses.* San Francisco, CA: Jossey-Bass.

Baumgarten, E. (1982). Ethics in the academic profession: A Socratic view. *Journal of Higher Education, 53,* 282–295.

Benjamin, E. (1996). Some implications of the faculty's obligation to encourage student academic freedom for faculty advocacy in the classroom. In P. M. Spacks (Ed.), *Advocacy in the classroom: Problems and possibilities* (pp. 302–314). New York, NY: St. Martin's Press.

Bennett, J. B. (1998). *Collegial professionalism: The academy, individualism, and the common good.* Phoenix, AZ: Oryx Press.

Bennett, J. B. (2003). *Academic life: Hospitality, ethics, and spirituality.* Bolton, MA: Anker.

Benton, T. H. (2004, February 6). Ignoring my inner lawyer. *The Chronicle of Higher Education*, p. C1.

Benton, T. H. (2004a, April 2). Remembering the old lions. *The Chronicle of Higher Education*, pp. C22–C23.

Benton, T. H. (2004b, August 3). On being a fat professor. *The Chronicle of Higher Education*, pp. C2–C3.

Benton, T. H. (December 9, 2005). Reference works and academic celebrity. *The Chronicle of Higher Education*, p. C1, C4.

Bergquist, W. H. (1992). *The four cultures of the academy: Insights and strategies for improving leadership in collegiate organizations.* San Francisco, CA: Jossey-Bass.

Bérubé, M. (1996). Professional advocates: When is "advocacy" part of one's vocation? In P. M. Spacks (Ed.), *Advocacy in the classroom: Problems and possibilities* (pp. 186–197). New York, NY: St. Martin's Press.

Bess, J. L. (1982). (Ed.). *New directions for teaching and learning: No. 10. Motivating professors to teach effectively.* San Francisco, CA: Jossey-Bass.

Blanco, M. (2005, October 14). Intelligent design and evolution in the classroom [Letter to the editor]. *The Chronicle of Higher Education*, pp. B13–B14.

Boyer, E. L. (1987). *College: The undergraduate experience in America.* San Francisco, CA: Jossey-Bass.

Brand, A. G. (1992). Drafting essay assignments: What the disciplines can learn from direct writing assessment. *Issues in Writing, 4*(2), 156–174.

Brookfield, S. D. (1991). *The skillful teacher: On technique, trust, and responsiveness in the classroom.* San Francisco, CA: Jossey-Bass.

Brossell, G. (1983). Rhetorical specification in essay examination topics. *College English, 45*(2), 165–173.

Brown, G., & Atkins, M. (1988). *Effective teaching in higher education.* London, U.K.: Methuen.

Brown, J. D., Hilgers, T., & Marsella, J. (1991). Essay prompts and topics: Minimizing the effect of mean differences. *Written Communication, 8*(3), 553–556.

Buchen, I. H. (1998). Servant leadership: A model for future faculty and future institutions. *Journal of Leadership Studies, 5*(1), 25–34.

Bush, L. R., III. (2005, October 14). Intelligent design and evolution in the classroom [Letter to the editor]. *The Chronicle of Higher Education,* p. B13.

Cahn, S. M. (1986). *Saints and scamps: Ethics in academia.* Totowa, NJ: Rowman & Littlefield.

Calhoun, S. (1996). A personal account of a struggle to be evenhanded in teaching about abortion. In P. M. Spacks (Ed.), *Advocacy in the classroom: Problems and possibilities* (pp. 365–371). New York, NY: St. Martin's Press.

Carlman, N. (1986). Topic differences on writing tests: How much do they matter? *English Quarterly, 19*(1), 39–49.

Chambers, C. M. (1983). The social contract nature of academic freedom. In M. C. Baca & R. H. Stein (Eds.), *Ethical principles, practices, and problems in higher education* (pp. 22–36). Springfield, IL: Charles C. Thomas.

Chickering, A. W., & Gamson, Z. F. (1987, March). Seven principles for good practice in undergraduate education. *AAHE Bulletin, 39*(7), 3–7.

Collins, W. (2005, October 14). Intelligent design and evolution in the classroom [Letter to the editor]. *The Chronicle of Higher Education*, p. B13.

Connell, M. A., & Savage, F. G. (1991). The role of collegiality in higher education tenure, promotion, and termination decisions. *Journal of College and University Law, 27*(4), 833–858.

Davis, B. G. (1993). *Tools for teaching.* San Francisco, CA: Jossey-Bass.

Davis, N. (1990). Sexual harassment in the university. In S. M. Cahn (Ed.), *Morality, responsibility, and the university: Studies in academic ethics* (pp. 150–176). Philadelphia, PA: Temple University Press.

Dewey, J. (1897, January). My pedagogic creed. *School Journal, 54*(3), 77–80.

Dewey, J. (1963). *Experience and education.* New York, NY: Collier Books. (Original work published 1938)

Dewey, J. (1966). *Democracy and education.* New York, NY: The Free Press. (Original work published 1916)

Dixon, N. (1996). The morality of intimate faculty-student relationships. *The Monist, 79*, 519–535.

Dudley-Evans, T. (1988). A consideration of the meaning of "discuss" in examination questions. In P. C. Robinson (Ed.), *Academic writing: Process and product* (pp. 47–52). Hong Kong: Modern English Publication, The British Council.

Dworkin, R. (1977). *Taking rights seriously.* Cambridge, MA: Harvard University Press.

Dziech, B. W., & Weiner, L. (1984). *The lecherous professor: Sexual harassment on campus.* Boston, MA: Beacon Press.

Eble, E. E. (1990). *The craft of teaching: A guide to mastering the professor's art* (2nd ed.). San Francisco, CA: Jossey-Bass.

Ericksen, S. C. (1984). *The essence of good teaching: Helping students learn and remember when they learn.* San Francisco, CA: Jossey-Bass.

Evans, C. (2004, June 18). What not to wear if you want to get on. *Times Higher Education Supplement,* p. 18.

Feldman, K. A. (1988). Effective college teaching from the students' and faculty's view: Matches or mismatched priorities? *Research in Higher Education, 28,* 291–344.

Findley, B. F., Jr. (1995). Teaching excellence: A reflective paradigm. *Community College Journal, 65*(4), 26–29.

Fish, S. (2003, May 16). Aim low. *The Chronicle of Higher Education,* p. C5.

Friedlander, M. (2005, October 14). Intelligent design and evolution in the classroom [Letter to the editor]. *The Chronicle of Higher Education,* p. B13.

Gallop, J. (1997). *Feminist accused of sexual harassment.* Durham, NC: Duke University Press.

Gewirth, A. (1990). Human rights and academic freedom. In S. M. Cahn (Ed.), *Morality, responsibility, and the university: Studies in academic ethics* (pp. 8–31). Philadelphia, PA: Temple University Press.

Gold, P. (1996). A teacher is either a witness or a stranger. In P. M. Spacks (Ed.), *Advocacy in the classroom: Problems and possibilities* (pp. 260–270). New York, NY: St. Martin's Press.

Greenberg, K. (1992). Some relationships between writing assignments and students' writing performance. *The Writing Instructor, 2,* 7–13.

Hauerwas, S. M. (1995). The morality of teaching. In A. L. DeNeef & C. D. Goodwin (Eds.), *The academic's handbook* (2nd ed., pp. 29–37). Durham, NC: Duke University Press.

Hendley, B. (1978). Martin Buber on the teacher/student relationship: A critical appraisal. *Journal of Philosophy of Education 12,* 141–148.

Higgins, C. (1998). Transference love from the couch to the classroom: A psychoanalytic perspective on the ethics of teacher-student romance. *Philosophy of Education Society Yearbook.* Retrieved from October 12, 2006, from: http://www.ed.uiuc.edu/eps/PES-Yearbook /1998/higgins.html

Hobson, E. H. (1998). Designing and grading written assignments. In R. S. Anderson & B. W. Speck (Eds.), *New directions for teaching and learning: No. 74. Changing the way we grade student performance: Classroom assessment and the new learning paradigm* (pp. 51–57). San Francisco, CA: Jossey-Bass.

Hoetker, J. (1982). Essay examination topics and students' writing. *College Composition and Communication, 33*(4), 377–392.

Hoetker, J., & Brossell, G. (1989). The effects of systematic variations in essay topics on the writing performance of college freshmen. *College Composition and Communication, 40*(4), 414–421.

Holmes, R. L. (1973). University neutrality and ROTC. *Ethics, 83,* 177–195.

Holmes, R. L. (1996). Sexual harassment and the university. *The Monist,* *79,* 499–518.

Hopkins-Powell, S. (2002, June 28). Opening ourselves to unconditional love in our relationships with students. *The Chronicle of Higher Education,* p. B5.

Huber, R. M. (1992). *How professors play the cat guarding the cream.* Fairfax, VA: George Mason University Press.

Hult, C. A. (1987). Assessment topics: The importance of rhetorical frame. *WPA: Writing Program Administration, 10*(3), 19–28.

Hutchings, P. (1996). *Making teaching community property: A menu for peer collaboration and peer review.* Washington, DC: American Association for Higher Education.

Hutchins, R. M. (1953). *The conflict in education in a democratic society.* New York, NY: Harper & Row.

Jackson, R. L., & Hagen, P. L. (2001). The ethics of faculty-student friendships. *Teaching Philosophy, 24*(1), 1–18.

Jefferson, T. (1964). Notes on the state of Virginia. New York, NY: Harper & Row. (Original work published 1781)

Johnson, N. J. (1998, March 6). The tie that binds: Peer pressure and dressing for academic success [Letter to the editor]. *The Chronicle of Higher Education,* p. B3.

Johnston, B. (1987). *Assessing English: Helping students reflect on their own work.* Philadelphia, PA: Open University Press.

Kant, I. (1997). Thoughts on education (A. Churton, Trans.). In S. M. Cahn (Ed.), *Classic and contemporary readings in the philosophy of education* (pp. 197–222). New York, NY: McGraw Hill.

Kinzer, C. K. (1987). Effects of topic and response variables on holistic score. *English Quarterly, 20*(2), 106–120.

Kipnis, L. (2004). Should students be allowed to hook up with professors? *Slate.* Retrieved October 12, 2006, from: http://slate.msn.com /id/2093351/

Kirby, S. C. (1987). Self-evaluation: A way to improve teaching and learning. *Teaching English in the Two-Year College, 14*(1), 41–46.

Kupperman, J. (1996). Autonomy and the very limited role of advocacy in the classroom. *The Monist, 79,* 488–498.

Lang, J. M. (2005, July 29). Looking like a professor. *The Chronicle of Higher Education,* pp. C2–C3.

Locke, J. (1997). Some thoughts concerning education. In S. M. Cahn (Ed.), *Classic and contemporary readings in the philosophy of education* (pp. 145–161). New York, NY: McGraw-Hill. (Original work published 1693)

Lost Budgie Blog. (2005). *Executed Chinese in Toronto body worlds show?* Retrieved October 12, 2006, from: http://lostbudgie.blogspot.com /2005/09/executed-chinese-in-toronto-body.html

Malloy, J. J. (1998, March 6). The tie that binds: Peer pressure and dressing for academic success [Letter to the editor]. *The Chronicle of Higher Education,* p. B3.

Markie, P. J. (1990). Professors, students, and friendship. In S. M. Cahn (Ed.), *Morality, responsibility, and the university: Studies in academic ethics* (pp. 134–149). Philadelphia, PA: Temple University Press.

Markie, P. J. (1994). *A professor's duties: Ethical issues in college teaching.* Lanham, MD: Rowman & Littlefield.

Markie, P. J. (1996). The limits of appropriate advocacy. In P. M. Spacks (Ed.), *Advocacy in the classroom: Problems and possibilities* (pp. 293–301). New York, NY: St. Martin's Press.

Martin, M. (1997). Advocating values: Professionalism in teaching ethics. *Teaching Philosophy, 1,* 19–34.

McNamara, M. J., & Deane, D. (1995). Self-assessment activities: Toward autonomy in language learning. *TESOL Journal, 5*(1), 17–21.

Menges, R. J., Weimer, M., & Associates. (1996). (Eds.). *Teaching on solid ground: Using scholarship to improve practice.* San Francisco, CA: Jossey-Bass.

Mill, J. S. (1989). *On liberty and other writings.* (S. Collini, Ed.). New York, NY: Cambridge University Press. (Original work published 1859)

Murphy, S., & Ruth, L. (1993). The field testing of writing prompts reconsidered. In M. Williamson & B. Huot (Eds.), *Validating holistic scoring for writing assessment: Theoretical and empirical foundations* (pp. 266–302). Cresskill, NJ: Hampton Press.

Myers, J., & Tronto, J. (1998). "Truth" and advocacy: A feminist perspective. *PS: Political Science and Politics, 31,* 808–810.

Nicholson, R. S. (1998, March 6). The tie that binds: Peer pressure and dressing for academic success [Letter to the editor]. *The Chronicle of Higher Education,* p. B3.

O'Brien, G. D. (1998). *All the essential half-truths about higher education.* Chicago, IL: The University of Chicago Press.

O'Donnell, H. (1984). ERIC/RCS report: The effect of topic on writing performance. *English Education, 16*(4), 243–249.

O'Donnell, A., & Dansereau, D. F. (1994). Learning from lectures: Effects of cooperative review. *Journal of Experimental Education, 61*(2), 116–125.

Perlmutter, D. D. (2004, December 10). Are we grading on the curves? *The Chronicle of Higher Education*, pp. B13-B14.

Pichaske, D. R. (1995, February 24). When students make sexual advances. *The Chronicle of Higher Education*, pp. B1–B2.

Plato. (1961). Republic. In E. Hamilton & H. Cairns (Eds.), *The collected dialogues of Plato* (pp. 575–844). Princeton, NJ: Princeton University Press.

Plato. (1980). Protagoras. In E. Hamilton & H. Cairns (Eds.), *The collected dialogues of Plato* (pp. 308–352). Princeton, NJ: Princeton University Press.

Powers, D. E., Fowles, M. E., Farnum, M., & Gerritz, K. (1992). *Giving a choice of topics on a test of basic writing skills: Does it make any difference?* Princeton, NJ: Educational Testing Service.

Rachels, J. (2003). *The elements of moral philosophy* (4th ed.). Boston, MA: McGraw-Hill.

Rawls, J. (1971). *A theory of justice.* Cambridge, MA: The President and Fellows of Harvard College.

Raymond, J. C. (1976). Cross-grading: An experiment in evaluating compositions. *College Composition and Communication, 27*(1), 52–55.

Rorty, R. (1989). Education without dogma: Truth, freedom, and our universities. *Dissent, 36*(2), 198–204.

Rosenberger *v.* Rector and Visitors of the University of Virginia, 515 U.S. 819 (1995).

Ross, W. D. (1930). *The right and the good.* Oxford, U.K.: Oxford University Press.

Roth, J. K. (Ed.). (1997). *Inspiring teaching: Carnegie professors of the year speak.* Bolton, MA: Anker.

Rousseau, J. (1979). *Emile* (A. Bloom, Trans.). New York, NY: Basic Books. (Original work published 1755)

Ruth, L., & Murphy, S. (1984). Designing topics for writing assessment: Problems of meaning. *College Composition and Communication, 35*(4), 410–422.

Ruth, L., & Murphy, S. (1998). *Designing writing tasks for the assessment of writing.* Norwood, NJ: Ablex.

Sawyer, R. K. (1998, March 6). The tie that binds: Peer pressure and dressing for academic success [Letter to the editor]. *The Chronicle of Higher Education,* p. B3.

Sawyer, T. M. (1975). Accountability: Or let others grade your students. *College Composition and Communication, 26*(4), 335–340.

Sawyer, T. M. (1976). External examiners: Separating teaching from grading. *Engineering Education, 66*(4), 344–346.

Scharton, M. (1989). Models of competence: Responses to a scenario writing assignment. *Research in the Teaching of English, 23*(2), 163–180.

Scharton, M. (1996). The politics of validity. In E. M. White, W. D. Lutz, & S. Kamusikiri (Eds.), *Assessment of writing: Politics, policies, practices* (pp. 53–75). New York, NY: Modern Language Association of America.

Schneider, A. (1998, January 23). Frumpy or chic? Tweed or kente? Sometimes clothes make the professor. *The Chronicle of Higher Education*, p. A12.

Shale, D. (1996). Essay reliability: Form and meaning. In E. M. White, W. D. Lutz, & S. Kamusikiri (Eds.), *Assessment of writing: Politics, policies, practices* (pp. 76–96). New York, NY: Modern Language Association of America.

Shapiro, J. (2005, October 14). Intelligent design and evolution in the classroom [Letter to the editor]. *The Chronicle of Higher Education*, p. B14.

Simon, R. L. (1994). *Neutrality and the academic ethic.* Lanham, MD: Rowman & Littlefield.

Snook. I. A. (Ed.). (1972). *Concepts of indoctrination: Philosophical essays.* London, U.K.: Routledge.

Speck, B. W. (1998). *Grading student writing: An annotated bibliography.* Westport, CT: Greenwood Press.

Speck, B. W. (2000). *Grading students' classroom writing: Issues and strategies* (ASHE-ERIC Higher Education Report, Vol. 27, No. 3). Washington, DC: George Washington University, Graduate School of Education and Human Development.

Speck, B. W. (2002). *Facilitating students' collaborative writing* (ASHE-ERIC Higher Education Report, Vol. 28, No. 6). New York, NY: Wiley.

Speck, B. W., & Jones, T. (1998). Direction in the grading of writing?: What the literature on the grading of writing does and doesn't tell us. In F. Zak & C. C. Weaver (Eds.), *The theory and practice of grading writing: Problems and possibilities* (pp. 17–29). New York, NY: State University of New York Press.

Sperber, M. (2005, September 9). Notes from a career in teaching. *The Chronicle of Higher Education*, pp. B20–B21.

Strike, K. A., & Soltis, J. F. (1998). *The ethics of teaching* (3rd ed.). New York, NY: Teachers College Press.

Superson, A. M. (2001). Amorous relationships between faculty and students. *The Southern Journal of Philosophy, 39*, 419–440.

Svinicki, M. D., & Menges, R. J. (1996). (Eds.). *New directions for teaching and learning: No. 65. Honoring exemplary teaching.* San Francisco, CA: Jossey-Bass.

Tennessee Senate Bill 1117. (2005). An act to amend Tennessee Code Annotated, Title 49, Chapter 7, relative to higher education.

Tom, A. (1997). The deliberate relationship: A frame for talking about faculty-student relationships. *The Alberta Journal of Educational Research, 43*(1), 3–21.

Tong, R. P. (1999). Feminist teachers, graduate students, and "consensual sex": Close encounters of a dangerous kind. *Teaching Philosophy, 22*(2), 123-133.

Tritt, M. (1983). Exchange grading with a workshop approach to the teaching of writing. *English Quarterly, 16*(1), 16–19.

Veith, G. E. (2005, October 8). Corpse art. *World, 20*(39), 30.

Wagner, E. N. (1993, May 26). Banning sexual fraternization. *The Chronicle of Higher Education*, pp. B1–B3.

Waks, J. D. (1998, March 6). The tie that binds: Peer pressure and dressing for academic success [Letter to the editor]. *The Chronicle of Higher Education*, p. B3.

Weaver, M. (1998). Weber's critique of advocacy in the classroom: Critical thinking and civic education. *PS: Political Science and Politics, 31,* 799–801.

White, J. O. (1988). Who writes these questions, anyway? *College Composition and Communication, 39,* 230–235.

Wilder, H. (1978). The philosopher as teacher: Tolerance and teaching philosophy. *Metaphilosophy, 9,* 311–323.

Wilhite, M. (1998, March 6). The tie that binds: Peer pressure and dressing for academic success [Letter to the editor]. *The Chronicle of Higher Education,* p. B3.

Willis, E. (2005, September 9). The pernicious concept of "balance." *The Chronicle of Higher Education,* p. B11.

Wolff, R. P. (1994). The myth of the neutral university. In R. L. Simon (Ed.), *Neutrality and the academic ethic* (pp. 103–109). Lanham, MD: Rowman & Littlefield.

Index